KNOWING THE LIVING GOD

KNOWING THE LIVING GOD

Roger Hazelton

The Judson Press, Valley Forge

KNOWING
THE LIVING
GOD

This book is a curriculum resource developed by the American Baptist
Board of Education and Publication in cooperation with the Christian
Churches (Disciples of Christ), the Church of the Brethren, the
Church of God (Anderson, Indiana), and All-Canada Baptist Publica-
tions.

Library of Congress Catalog Card No. 69-11679

The Judson Press, Valley Forge, Pa. 19481
Printed in the U.S.A.

Preface

In these days it takes a certain amount of boldness, or maybe only stubbornness, to write another book about God. Yet it has recently been said — by a theologian, of course — that the question about God is "the only question there is." Even allowing for the occupational shortsightedness of such a statement, something in it deserves to be heard and heeded. Can we have grasped the peculiar quality of the time in which we are living unless we recognize that sounding through all the other doubts which people are expressing is the doubt about God? Perplexities concerning war and peace, power and justice, revolution and renewal, all point beyond themselves to a prior problem: In what do we finally trust — where do we put our last and best hope? That search, whatever path it follows, is the quest for God.

This brief book, accordingly, seeks to raise once more the possibility of God as a "live option" for thoughtful people of today. While it does not pretend to contain all or even most of the answers, it is written out of a concern that a lively faith in a living God can be mightily helpful in coping with the problems that beset us all. Therefore in this book we shall be thinking together about what such faith in God involves, what it asks of us, and where it may be expected to lead us.

Although the book bears the name of a single author, it is actually the outcome of consultation and conversation with many colleagues in the Cooperative Curriculum Project. They have given me the benefit of their experience and criticism, which I gratefully acknowledge. I must, however, accept full responsibility for the form in which this interdenominational venture is cast. The book serves as a basic resource of the perspective "Knowing the Living God," which represents the first year of a curriculum plan, developed cooperatively by several denominations: the American Baptist Board of Education and Publication, the Christian Churches (Disciples of Christ), the Church of the Brethren, the Church of God (Anderson, Indiana), and the All-Canada Baptist Publications. The volume is written for general reading by all people seeking to think about the theological dimensions of life.

Just who are teachers and who are learners in the contemporary church is difficult to say. The time of one-way communication from the institution to the individual is surely past. Old traditions of believing are encountering new ways of perceiving and being in the world. But for that very reason it may be important to place present-day anxieties and queries concerning God within the longer, larger perspective of man's unending seeking after God. That such a search has been and will again be rewarded is perhaps the deepest conviction of this book. No Christian ever claimed that belief is easy or that faith comes naturally; yet it is also the heart of our faith that those who truly seek shall surely find, and this assurance should encourage and engage us all.

ROGER HAZELTON

Contents

1

Faith at first or second hand?

How may we, as men and women of our time, come to know the living God? To help in finding an answer to that question is the purpose of this book. It is part of a larger venture in Christian education in which many teachers and writers are cooperating. All are firmly committed to the conviction that such a task as this is imperative and wholly practical. We are gratefully aware of the lessons and resources that are available within the Christian heritage, and yet our major interest lies in bringing that heritage to life for those to whom a lively faith in God no longer comes easily or naturally in today's changing world.

Surely it will not come without questioning and searching for any one of us. Faith in the God who speaks and acts in the midst of life is no longer something to be taken merely for granted. It must be the fruit of careful thought, fashioned out of real experiences and genuine concerns, patiently and honestly reached. This book is planned for those who are willing and ready to take part in that kind of endeavor.

Our purpose, simply put, is to show how the faith of our fathers, "the faith," may become our own faith as fully as it was theirs.

Faith as Firsthand Experience

How many members of churches seem content with what can only be called a secondhand faith! Such people want to be known as Christians, but without knowing personally what being Christian means and demands. So they tend to stand on doctrines or practices inherited from the past, as if the lines were long ago laid down and needed only to be dutifully followed. Who are we, they ask, to suppose that we can improve upon our fathers' and forefathers' faith in God? Is it not safe to assume that the Bible or perhaps the ancient creeds, reinforced by later statements of the church's faith, tell us all we need to know and ought to believe?

Now of course this reliance upon past achievements and interpretations is not altogether wrong. After all, the Christian faith was not born yesterday. Men and women have gone this way before us, leaving behind their cherished testimony to the God who revealed himself in Christ. We are surely right in wanting to understand and accept for ourselves the truth they discovered, proclaimed, and lived. Every time we ask the meaning of a passage of Scripture, or participate in the Lord's Supper, or seek Christian light upon the tangled issues of contemporary living, we express our very real dependence on those who have gone before us in the pilgrimage of faith.

Yet even as we express that dependence and bear our tribute in the continuing Christian community from generation to generation, we know that something more is required of us. We are not a genealogical society congratulating ourselves on being the descendants of our ancestors. True, a secondhand, inherited faith may do for a start, and that is where most of us begin anyway. But there come times of personal anxiety and testing, or of profound cultural change and shock, when faith at second hand is not enough and cannot stand the strain life puts upon it. Then too, even in the normal, gradual course of human growth, old beliefs and values yield to new ones, as they should. "As you were" is no rule for growing up into genuine maturity of faith, or of life in general. Any person who is capable of responding to the claims of increased knowledge and advancing experience will be drawn inevitably into the process of questioning and searching which this book is written to encourage.

So let us not confuse true faith with its secondhand substitute. That would be at best a kind of mental and spiritual laziness, letting matters ride, allowing others to do our believing instead of doing our own. And at worst, it would amount to a grinning mockery of all that Christian faith actually means, refusing to do more than go through the bare motions of worship, belief, and service in Christ's name. When this occurs, as it all too often does, faith has been turned into its very opposite — the tired and outworn repetition of things which one has not yet earned his right to say.

But if God is ever to become our present help and Jesus Christ our own true Lord, then it is plain that a faith at first, not second hand will have to be discovered. As Martin Luther put it, each of us must do his own believing just as each must do his own dying. It is as serious as that. Christian faith can never be a purely private matter, but it is a deeply personal one. That is why the Apostles' Creed, which is said together by the congregation in some churches, begins with the first-person singular, "I believe." Faith in order to be shared must first of all become one's own. To live in a community of faith means that one accepts responsibility for taking that faith with personal seriousness.

There is a further reason why the subject of this book, *Knowing the Living God*, is challenging and timely. To be quite honest about it, is not belief in a God who lives very much of an open question today? Our children are introduced into a world which goes about its business as if there were no God, or at least not a God who makes any apparent difference to the way people talk, feel, or act. They cannot be blamed for drawing their own conclusions about that. In our churches, it is true, a kind of "rumor" that there is a God is still kept in circulation. But like old songs nostalgically sung, the "rumor" is cherished more for its dear familiarity than for any fresh insight it may bring to the living of our days. All too evidently, the world is going down a different road, dancing to a different tune, from which the signs of a living God are conspicuously missing.

In such a situation it cannot be a matter simply of telling people what we think they ought to believe, in spite of everything they see to the contrary. Neither is it to be supposed that if only Christians speak, the world will be bound to listen. Least of all can we expect that "this too will pass" and an age of splendid, shining belief in God will automatically follow once the world has come to its senses. No, the burden of proof now lies plainly with those who say they believe in God. The "rumor" that there is a God will, in the last resort, be either confirmed or denied by what Christians themselves can know and show of God.

Faith as Creative Encounter

How does the migration from secondhand report to firsthand experience of God take place? If we could have the answer in terms of a technique that guaranteed arrival, it would be a fairly simple matter to set up the proper instruments and follow the correct methods. Indeed, some have tried to make man's search for a knowledge of the living God a business of rules and regulations which, if carefully observed, would assure success. It is a perennial temptation in all religion to want to control the means of access to God, whether through revivalistic preaching, proper indoctrination of the young, or sacramental observance. Each group has its own way of guaranteeing safe conduct to the place where God may be found while frowning at the ways used by others.

But if anything is clear to those of us who have been nourished in the faith of the Bible it is that God cannot be counted upon to be where men would like to find him. When men seek to house him in the temple they have built to his glory, God destroys the temple. When they try to make of him a tribal or a national deity, God may answer by handing his people over to their enemies. And when religion would confine God in its institutions, rituals, Scriptures, or ethics, God breaks out of bounds and confronts men in the everyday world. The one thing of which we can be sure is that we cannot be sure of God, on our terms and according to our methods. That is just because he is a living God who himself sets the terms on which men may come to know him.

This is the first point to be borne in mind as we inquire into the character of firsthand faith and the processes within experience that may lead us toward it. God, whatever else he may be or do, is his own kind of God. He takes priority over all man-made definitions of his reality; he seizes the initiative in approaching us, not least in the channels of religion; he cannot be pinned down or counted upon to meet our expectations; and even as we speak of him most humbly and wonderingly he breaks through our language and escapes. This is not because God is playing games with us or delights in mystifying us, but because he wills to be God in his relationship to us. So, when Moses asked the name of the God who spoke to him out of the burning bush, he received this answer: "I am who I am." Faith at first hand always has this character of a mysterious meeting, a decisive encounter, with the living God.

But does this mean that there is nothing to be done on our part other than listening and waiting for God to reveal who he is? Hardly, for even waiting and listening are highly concentrated forms of human activity, which can be learned and practiced. To acquire that intentness, that capacity for discernment which is the sign of human readiness for God's self-revealing — this is a very worthy, important task. There are minds to be opened to the truth of God, spirits to be freed for the touch of God. There are meanings to be expressed and communicated, experiences to be encouraged and valued, relationships to be established and sustained. All this is man's work to be done, it is true, for the glory of God; yet the doing of it demands gifts and skills of many sorts which we can exercise capably and cooperatively.

Faith comes to us for the most part through the existing channels of teaching, preaching, and worship in the church and the family. What we know of God is first of all what we hear others say about him. One may indeed hope that this knowledge will be much revised and enlarged at a later stage of the learner's development, providing opportunities for his growth, correction, and more comprehensive understanding. Faith is not a fixed point but a pilgrimage; nevertheless it is important where the journey begins. Christian nurture does not merely aim to perpetuate Christianity from generation to generation, although self-preservation is of course necessary if the greater work of the church in witness and mission is to be carried on. Christian nurture, however, is the church engaged in a process of initiating its members into those experiences and meanings which give promise of enlarging and deepening their life-faith. To this end it calls upon the available resources within the existing Christian community.

We are well aware today that the movement from inherited and imitative religious behavior to a firsthand, personally held faith is by no means automatic. The time is long past when information or indoctrination in so-called Christian subjects could be expected to yield life-changing results. All the same, a stable medium for Christian learning and doing is obviously necessary; a substantial web of meanings and experiences, built up out of centuries of church tradition, must be placed at the disposal of teachers and learners alike. To suppose that this web is a closed system or a fixed pattern, needing only to be accepted and applied by those who come under its influence, is sadly to misjudge both its real force and the way in which human beings actually respond and grow.

The danger always is that faith will be directed to the symbol rather than to the reality it seeks to express, to the witness instead of that to which it witnesses. Honoring the flag is meaningless if no real patriotism is behind it. Saying "Lord, Lord" is no substitute for having Christ as Lord of one's life. Man, it seems, has an inveterate tendency to "embalm life alive" in shapes, which under the pretext of making faith easier only makes it the more unlikely. The work of the sensitive interpreter or skillful teacher thus becomes that of extricating faith from its entombment in religiosity, perhaps even smashing a few cherished idols along the way, for the sake of genuine interaction between available resource and desired response, between the gospel and the world of present human relationships and responsibilities. Only as this kind of contact is made does conventional religion become creative faith.

Faith as Venture and Trust

How shall we describe this goal of the nurturing process in the church? Recognizing that it is far easier to define true faith than to acquire it, we, nevertheless, will be helped if we keep our ultimate direction in view. Faith in God, as understood by Christians through the centuries, has naturally been described in a wide variety of ways. Most superficially and, alas, most generally, faith has been thought of as assent or obedience, the one related to biblical or doctrinal assertions, the other related to rules for conduct and specifications for character. The essence of both ways of viewing faith is conformity with ready-made standards, agreement with answers found "in the back of the book" — standards and answers thought sufficient to cover every situation and authoritative because divinely given or ordained. This is what may be called the popular or vulgar notion of faith, whether Protestant or Catholic.

That it is no more than a caricature of Christian faith is obvious, of course; but we should not underestimate its influence in Christian circles even today. "Only believe" or "keep the faith" means, with dismal frequency, thinking or doing as one is told. And have not Christians always admonished each other to "guard" the faith, from the time of the earliest pastoral letters until now? This certainly suggests that faith is something to be preserved intact — received as a legacy and handed down to those who come after, rather like a choice piece of antique furniture.

This view makes real sense, to be sure, in times of persecution or exile from the home base when sheer survival is important. It does not, however, have the same force when the danger threatening Christians is rather that of comfortable approval, pious irrelevance, and nostalgia for a simpler, safer state of affairs. Then, indeed, hardening faith into propositions claiming assent, or moralizing and legalizing it into commands to be obeyed, is actually an act of treason against faith itself. What we are left with is the dry rot of faith and not its living and life-giving plant. We want to control our faith, not to be controlled by it.

Faith, in order to be faith, needs constantly to be renewed at its source. Instead of taking a position or holding a line, it is best understood as keeping open to the possibility of new life set before us in Christ, looking eagerly and loyally to him who is the author and finisher of our faith. All the doctrines and requirements thrown up in the course of Christian history cannot produce such faith, and exist only to encourage and enlist it.

But we are still speaking of "faith" as if we knew all along exactly what it means; and this is hardly the case. Without presuming to define faith with anything like finality, ought we not at least attempt to be as clear as possible regarding it? We do not lack significant clues and models from Scripture and Christian experience; on the contrary, we have these clues in abundance, and they are indispensable to our own understanding.

One mark of a life lived in faith is its *mobility*. This word is used most often at present to signify rapid and frequent change of location, which is perhaps not a bad point at which to begin. Why is Abraham accounted the human father of our biblical and Christian faith? Because he was the ancestor of so many descendants, as numerous as the sands on the shore or the stars in heaven? Partly, but mostly because when called by God he "went forth, not knowing whither he was to go." It was Abraham's mobility that set in motion the age-long pilgrimage of the people of God. It was his movement away from the tried and the true toward a truth that had not yet been tried which has made him our companion and our example in the life of faith. Willingness to be changed, made new, in answer to a call regarded as coming from God — this is utterly basic to a truly personal faith. When it is present in a human being by the grace of God, it is a sign not so much that a man has faith as that faith has him.

Every day is moving day in the Christian life. Although like Abraham, we do not know what it may bring forth, we move through it with expectancy and urgency, intent upon seizing its opportunities and meeting its challenges. To live by faith, as John Bunyan expressed it so unforgettably, is then to be a pilgrim, a wayfaring stranger, in constant, purposeful motion through the scenes and stages of our human experience. It is not mobility for its own sake that characterizes the Christian pilgrimage of faith, however. We are not religious hoboes bumming our way through the world. The point is that we cannot live our faith without making the decision, in Martin Luther's great words, to "Let goods and kindred go, this mortal life also" in order that the sense of divine distance and destination may control us.

Hence a second, and deeper, sign of faith is *venture in commitment.* The unsettling and shaking of old foundations is its condition, but God's promise of new being, his invitation extended in Jesus Christ, is its cause. Faith is by no means a "sure thing" if this denotes a rule of safety or a guarantee of arrival at some prearranged goal. There is risk in faith because it respects and demands our freedom, with all its ambiguity and uncertainty. Believing in God does not foreclose the issues of life but opens and enriches them. When the psalmist shouts, "My heart is fixed, O God, my heart is fixed," he means that wherever he goes he will go with God, whatever he must face he will face it with God.

Trust in God — that is without doubt the most inward, personally essential mark of faith. How often, though, it is confused with mere submission on the one hand, or with bare performance of duty on the other! Neither by itself can possibly express the full human texture of Christian faith. There are times when we have to submit, it is true, just as there are times when we ought to act; but faith as trust in God includes more than either of these. To give our lives into God's gracious keeping will certainly involve both taking things as they come and acting without knowing. At bottom, however, it means letting God be God, our God, by putting ourselves at his disposal and making way for him to act in us. Faith therefore means that assent is deepened into obedience and obedience is enlarged into loyalty; it means putting our trust in the eminently trustworthy God who loved and loves us still in Jesus Christ.

Faith as Possession of Our Heritage

We have been speaking of the difference between first-hand and secondhand faith, and of the way from the latter to the former. No one can give the chart for another's journey, and yet there is impressive corporate testimony to the nature of God's claim in Christ and man's appropriate reply — testimony which will be described and drawn upon in the following chapters. A vast multitude of people have taken this "journey not of feet," as Saint Augustine called it. They seem sometimes to have little in common by way of human qualities; they can hardly be brought under any one heading of parallel development or of standardized behavior, for they are a various and sundry lot of people like ourselves. Yet they are joined together at a deeper level and their oneness is all the more remarkable because it is in keeping with so many differences. There is such a group in man's history — let us confess it gladly — as the communion of saints. Their unity is found precisely in their common fidelity and loyalty. It is the very opposite of humanly imposed uniformity of belief or behavior. It consists simply in the truth of the affirmation: "We are Christians; we belong to Christ."

Without continuity in history there can be no real human community, but only temporary associations on a short-term, emergency basis. What the British poet T. S. Eliot termed "the backing of the dead" is indispensable for all the deeper and more durable forms of man's togetherness in the world. And Christian faith exhibits such a continuity in unmistakable, highly significant degree.

Recently Protestantism, under the stimulus of Roman Catholic renewal, has been rediscovering the importance of tradition in the process by which others' faith becomes our own. Now we can see as perhaps never before how corporate and historical all Christian faith actually is. Biblical scholars have shown how the books of the New Testament, for example, are the result of apostolic memory, proclamation, and worship, so that the Bible is in fact tradition before it is Scripture.

Tradition, however, is itself ambiguous. It means "handing down" the crystallized experiences of Christian men and women from one generation to the next, as the original gospel is cherished and communicated from parent to child, teacher to learner, pastor to congregation, group to person. Indeed, every effort toward renewal or reformation, far from simply being a break with the immediate past, is an appeal to a more remote and normative past. We trace our lineage back to the primitive Christian community and even beyond that to the earthly life and teaching of the Lord Jesus himself. It is both inevitable and right that we should do so. The true "apostolic succession" is to be found within the living continuity of faith expressed in every congregation of God's people when a hymn is sung, the Bible read, prayer offered, or a sermon preached. It is also expressed, no less emphatically, in Christian action motivated by neighborly and brotherly love in the spirit of Jesus.

But tradition may mean something else. The Christian faith is never found in a pure state. It appears in ancient history buttressed by the military power of the Roman Empire, in contemporary Asian countries as a Western import, in the pluralistic setting of the modern secular city as a self-perpetuating institution. It is as if our faith could not be "handed down" without at the same time being "handed over" to the culture into which it comes. Yes, Judas is tempted to betray Jesus with a kiss of hypocritical reverence in every generation.

What then can be done to reawaken firsthand faith while maintaining continuity with our rightly treasured heritage? Only as we take "the leap of faith" ourselves, in the time and place which God has given us, can the insidious temptation to conventional imitation and piecemeal borrowing be avoided. The most unbiblical thing we can do is to copy out Bible maxims and proof-texts to justify the churchly status quo. The most unchristian attitude that can be imagined is the idolization of Christ, saying "Lord, Lord," while refusing to meet him at the center of our own life.

To put our faith not in someone else's faith, but rather in that which called forth his faith, is what being Christian means. There is a rendezvous with the gospel which each of us must keep. There is a living God to be known still, as he was known of old, in the dense and cluttered experiences of daily life. It is to this task of discernment and decision that we are called today.

What is the importance of right beliefs in developing a firsthand faith? What makes a belief "right?"

What further examples of the "embalming" or "freezing" process can be seen at work in Christianity today?

What specific suggestions would you have for applying the "creative" principle to the normal services of worship in your church?

What reasons do you have for agreeing — or disagreeing — with the author that "the Bible is in fact tradition before it is Scripture"?

2

Knowing and being known

Our age, it seems, is pretty well dominated by what has been called the triumph of the fact. Is it not true that by and large we are fact-minded, not to say fact-happy and fact-obsessed? More and more, education has become a kind of data processing in which facts are transferred from one brain to another. We easily confuse statistics with significance, and put great trust in the virtue of mere information masquerading as intelligence. All this has profound bearing upon the very notion of what "knowing" means to us, and places a special burden upon those who dare to speak of knowing God.

God Is Not a Fact

Whatever else he may be, God is obviously not a fact. He does not turn up at the other end of microscopes or telescopes. He escapes our nets of detection; no radar screen has yet been devised which can pick up his presence in the world. Space probes yield no inkling of his whereabouts. Indeed, the more refined and far-ranging our techniques of fact-finding become, the less likely it is that they will discover anything at all remotely resembling God.

Does this mean, then, that knowledge of God is strictly

impossible? Must God be relegated to the discarded heap of outworn fables and exploded superstitions? Many in our world believe that this is so, and they are not all atheistic communists either. The question of God is simply a question of evidence, some say, and, if evidence of a factual kind is lacking, then the matter is decided negatively. It is as simple, and as devastating, as that.

This conclusion appears plausible on the ground that knowledge of facts is the only kind of knowledge there is. This idea has been greatly furthered by the spectacular successes of science in our modern world. Have we not all seen and benefited from the observations and discoveries of scientists who were willing to let the facts speak for themselves without the distortions caused by private preference or cultural bias? Can we ever be grateful enough for the advance of scientific knowledge which has placed within our power the possibility of overcoming man's ancient enemies of disease, ignorance, and poverty? Has not all this happened because scientists determined to dispense with "the hypothesis of God" in their investigations and explanations of the natural world, permitting only what can be seen, handled, or measured to be regarded as known?

Nevertheless, in the development of modern science some fateful misunderstanding seems to have been at work — the notion that reality itself can be shrunk to the size of the known or the knowable, and that truth can only mean what is verified scientifically. The immense prestige of science, as well as its undoubted benefits for all mankind, has encouraged and tended to harden this notion. More often generally assumed than stated outright, it has become almost a kind of modern dogma — a dogma which scientists themselves have not hesitated to call unscientific.

Knowledge Is More than Fact

The sway of this "scientific" dogma has certainly been giving the Christian faith a hard time. In reply to it Christian believers in God have two important things to say. The first is that of course God is not a fact, or pattern of facts, which can be detected and in some fashion controlled within the physical universe; our faith has never claimed this. The second thing to be said is that there is more than one kind of knowledge, for man makes response to the real on more than one level of his existence, and therefore to rule out God and faith in him altogether is both premature and presumptuous.

For consider: if factual, scientific knowledge is all the knowledge there is or ever can be, then by what right do we call it knowledge? It would seem that it meets certain standards which it cannot itself create but only illustrate. And if reality is exclusively material and measurable, then what is truly real about it? Surely the judgment that something is real is made upon a broader base and a different ground than facts alone can provide. Just as our experience is greater than our knowledge, so truth is wider and deeper than the realm of facts. The way is still open for an interpretation of both truth and knowledge more in harmony with the undying assurances of our Christian faith in God.

There is more than one method or model of knowledge, and science itself proves this. Careful observation, accurate measurement, reasoned argument, together with more personal qualities like tentativeness, empathy, and insight, all enter into scientific work and make its harvest of knowledge possible. For science is above all else a human enterprise, calling into play those skills and energies of which man's spirit is capable, and carried on when all is said and done for frankly human ends. He who would use science as an argument against faith is barking up the wrong tree, as the saying goes, because science is a most impressive example of the use of faith, if this means readiness to trust and commit oneself beyond the evidence at hand.

Therefore any effort to straitjacket the many ways men have of knowing our many avenues to truth and reality into only one way will not do. Just as we live on more than one level at once, so we meet the world around us in a great variety of ways. It is important, if only for the sake of being sane, to distinguish what is so from what we only fancy, fear, or wish for; but this cannot be done merely by supposing that all knowledge is of one particular type. The truth of the matter is far more complicated than that. There is a whole spectrum of ways of knowing and a many-leveled reality to be known. This is where our thinking about "knowing the living God" must begin.

Knowing Ourselves and Each Other

With all due respect to science, there are instances of knowledge which are not scientific but personal and interpersonal. These do not belong on that account to a lower grade or degree of knowledge; they are simply different and must be seen and valued as such. In some respects, personal and interpersonal knowledge may be regarded as higher and fuller than that supplied by science, because the former involves us more completely and radically than the latter. If it is a fact that I want to know, I must keep my distance, remain "objective" at all costs, become as "impersonal" as possible. But if it is a person whom I wish to know, I am caught up in an "I-thou relationship" in which I have to declare and commit myself if such knowledge is to occur. For here the "object" of my search is another "subject" like myself; knowledge of persons can be given to us only as we give ourselves to them. "All real life is meeting," as Martin Buber said.

The facts that chemistry or sociology can teach us about ourselves and others are undoubtedly significant; but when they have been learned there is still a venture of trust and self-confiding to be made before our knowledge at the fully human level is complete, useful, or decisive for character and conduct. How may I verify the friendliness of my neighbor except by acting toward him in a friendly manner? Or how may I prove that my wife is faithful to me except by having faith in her? Here words like "prove" and "verify" have quite clearly a different sort of meaning from that employed in scientific or factual knowledge. This is because they have to do with a basically different zone or dimension of the real.

Perhaps what we are trying to point out can be said in another way. All personal knowledge is at bottom interpersonal. That is, its chief requirement is a mutual give-and-take, an openness one to another, which makes all the difference between knowing the facts about someone and knowing him as he is. Indeed, I only come to know myself through others' knowledge of me, as it is reflected in their manner of approach toward me. If we cannot see ourselves as others see us, we can at least see ourselves in their seeing of us; and the same holds for them as well.

Or let us try still a third tack: knowing and being known as persons are but two sides of a single human event. It is relationship at the human and not merely the factual level that makes this possible. I must take responsibility for entering into it, sustaining it, and deepening it as occasions arise. As one contemporary thinker puts it, I must place myself at the disposal of the other, and this will be the avenue of his approach to me; otherwise, the gate of personal knowledge is firmly shut. But the other side of this important truth is this: the other person is known to me only if he chooses to be known, and so far as he chooses to be known. I cannot wrest his secret from him if he does not wish to reveal it, for he is not simply a thing but a person like myself.

How God May Be Known

What has just been said is indispensable for getting at the personal, in contrast to the merely factual, element in the spectrum of knowledge. Building on it as a sure foundation, we may open up the matter of our knowledge of God. For if anything is clear, it is that God is to be known as persons are, not facts, and that what is imperative for knowing him is self-commitment on our part and a willingness to let God speak his own Word about himself. Our models for understanding and entering into the knowledge of God are to be drawn, then, from the personal and interpersonal realm of all knowledge.

This is not because God is a person exactly like ourselves, but rather because of the deeply personal and interpersonal nature of our faith in him. The ways in which the Bible, for example, describes God are those of speaking, willing, acting, and feeling which are familiarly human. Words like these have to be used because they alone do justice to the kind of meeting they are meant to describe. Since we are involved with God on these deep levels of our being, it does not make sense to think of God as a fact or an axiom. For if God could be simply taken for granted as a force like electricity or as a body of truth like mathematics, he would not be what faith knows him to be — the living Lord who calls us into his service and rightfully claims our whole obedience to his will.

There are moments, however, in our religious experience when personal and interpersonal terms fail us. Then they are neither spacious nor accurate enough to set forth the scope and depth of God's dealings with us or the manner of our relationship to him. At such times our analogies for God must be drawn from the natural rather than the human world. So in the Bible the spirit of God is pictured as a mighty rushing wind, and the grace of God is compared with sunshine or springtime. If indeed we have to do with God at all, it is not as if we were involved with someone like ourselves, only greater and better. When men speak seriously or meaningfully of God they are bound to find words of human likeness indispensable, but also at some points inadequate.

It is important for people of our time to understand this, because we tend to use the language of human intercourse almost exclusively regarding God. Our instinct is to leave nature to the scientists while concentrating upon what is uniquely human in God's manner of acting and being. We strongly prefer dramatic words of personal encounter and response to those expressing the processes and structures that underlie life, make it possible, and give to it what the theologian Paul Tillich called "ultimacy of concern."

Assuredly we have to do in Christian faith with one who calls and claims us for himself, whose ways with men may therefore properly be described in terms of our most characteristic and decisive human experience. Yet it is also our faith that this same God who keeps covenant with us, willing and working for our salvation, is the maker of heaven and earth as well. He can only be our God because he is in the first place "Lord of the universe," in the phrase from a Jewish prayer — because, in short, he is God in his own right and reality, far exceeding human grasp or likeness.

Knowing God, then, may rightly be compared with the ways in which we know ourselves and each other, since no lesser tokens can possibly convey the divine approach and the human answer which our faith wishes to describe. But this is not to say that these are enough. They should be supplemented and enlarged by other images of that reality which surrounds and upholds man. God is not less, but more, than personal. While we cannot do without the personal in our thought of him, we should not limit our thought to what is merely personal. If the knowledge of God must begin at the level of human meeting and involvement, it cannot end there.

There are always dangers and difficulties in any effort to say what God is like, but they are greater in speaking of God impersonally than in speaking of him personally. Perhaps the best rule to follow is that while we operate, as of course we must, from a human base, we should try to fill out and deepen our thought of God by reference to more-than-human levels of the real, if we are not to end up with a pseudo-God who is no more than the projection of our own imaginings and strivings. In thinking of God, the personal and interpersonal are primary, but not total. Our minds must make a place for the God whose thoughts are not our thoughts and whose ways, when all is said and done, are not our ways.

Knowledge According to Our Faith

Faith in God, as it appears in the Bible, does not regard him as an object to be uncovered after long search in a final act called "knowledge." Rather, this faith understands God to be the Subject or Knower who is forever searching out man, making man his "object," so to speak. And in the same perspective man comes to know himself as he is known by God, looking forward to the time when he shall know even as he is known at present. Since this is a striking departure from the usual way in which we think of knowing in our modern world, it deserves a careful look.

In the first place, how does man reach personal and social maturity? Is it not through broadening the range of his awareness, moving from self-centeredness toward responsible concern for others? None of us can avoid seeing the world from his particular vantage point, according to his own interests, needs, and heritage. I do not step out of my own skin or abandon altogether my center of reference when I realize that I am only one among many selves which view the world from centers other than mine. Faith in God does not ask me to stop being myself; it does however require of me the grace to see myself as others see me, as a member of a common humanity of unique persons. That is the point behind the "as thyself" which is at the heart of the Golden Rule given by Jesus. In it our Lord admits, and shows us how to overcome, the inevitable self-centeredness in all our experience. Living my own life thus becomes living for others, and my life is strangely fulfilled and found to the extent in which it is expended for the common good.

All this is doubtless true, someone may say, but what does it have to do with knowledge? Just this: knowledge, after all, is a distinctively human happening taking place according to the forms and processes of human growth generally. This means among other things that every knower is himself a factor in his knowing, not to be disregarded in any account of it that claims to be adequate. A powerful electronic microscope may change very small objects by the light it sheds on them. Man's knowledge, too, is colored and determined in large part by the knower's image of himself, as well as by his interpersonal involvement.

For too long in the modern world, knowledge has been considered in a framework that is basically subhuman. It has been confused with data processing of the computer type or with a camera-like recording of available facts. That is to give an account of knowledge which is far too minimal and meager. The human element is missing. The knower has been made to vanish from his knowledge.

What is needed, therefore, is most assuredly the rehumanizing of knowledge. The act of knowing is far more than accumulating information; it is an expression of our personal and corporate humanness. Accurate observing and disinterested recording, however important in themselves, make up only part of the process called knowing. It rests also upon the exercise of gifts like sympathy and insight, and of virtues such as patience and self-forgetfulness. Its laws are those of human growth itself, which takes place within the context of shared response to a many-leveled reality. Without denying for a moment that there is indeed an element of sheer seeing of what is there, a kind of confrontation in all knowledge, it is still true that the knower himself is not to be ignored.

In the second place, the biblical faith in a God who can be known is made clearer if we recognize the active, dynamic role of God in making such knowledge possible. For it is not as if God were an inert, passive object waiting to be ferreted out by human ingenuity or resourcefulness. No; our faith is that God makes the first move toward us, that he wills to make himself known, so that as we go in search of him we find him meeting us more than halfway. Faith's first lesson is that I am not the center of my world, but God is. I have to do with God even when I prefer to be left undisturbed and unaroused. He visits me on his terms, not mine. If it is peace I want, he brings me a sword. If I look for him in the thunder, he comes in a still, small voice. This is but to say that God is not an object but a Subject, a Knower like myself, and that he cannot be known unless he wills to be.

And by the same token, when God is not known it is because he hides himself, as the Bible puts it, which means that God retains control over our manner of approaching him. "Canst thou by searching find out God?" The answer to this biblical question must be "No." We simply do not have "what it takes" to produce the conditions for knowing God on our own; and if we are unable to know him, the reasons similarly lie beyond our human power. Whether he is known or unknown, and in whatever manner or degree, is finally within God's purpose and not man's.

Faith in God does not depend upon our having knowledge of him, but our knowledge is according to our faith. Something like direct and personal acquaintance with God, however imperfect or faltering, precedes and makes possible any knowledge we may have of him. We do not begin by developing correct doctrines and clear ideas concerning God, and only then relate ourselves to him in personal fellowship. Instead, we start with awareness and grow on toward comprehension, as we do in all our living. I cannot know what fatherhood means except within the actual experience of relationship to my own father. So my knowledge of God, meager or full as it may be, rests back upon that willingness to trust God with the issues of my life — which is called faith. Of course, the difference between knowing my father and coming to know God is that I may one day become a father myself and thus understand fatherhood from the inside, while God is by nature beyond such human possibility of knowing. We may share in the life of God but we cannot live that life; and although we may grow in understanding God it will not be within our power to know him with either the intimacy or completeness of our own self-knowledge.

Yet there is a third consideration regarding the biblical viewpoint which ought to hearten us for the venture of knowing the living God. It is this: in faith we are not merely would-be knowers but committed believers who have already made our choice and taken our stand with God. Not that we ever have enough of God, at least in this life, to satisfy our thirst for absolute certainty or final truth! Human experience, even at its highest and best, is wrapped in what the mystics call a "cloud of unknowing." But when this has been said, it needs to be added that to know in part is far better than not to know at all. The man of faith who cries out in the Psalms, "My heart is fixed, O God, my heart is fixed," is voicing his assurance of the sufficiency of God. He knows in whom he believes; he neither claims nor needs any greater knowledge.

It is possible to overemphasize the fragmentary, incomplete knowledge of God vouchsafed to faith in such a way that beginners in the Christian life may be discouraged from going further. Then "one step enough for me" becomes a rule of resignation, not advance. This tendency is most pronounced in a fact-minded time like ours when object-knowledge may seem to be the only kind of knowledge there is.

It is therefore good to realize that while believing is not knowing in the fullest sense, it is not mere guesswork either. When Abraham "went out, not knowing where he was to go," his faith in God more than made up for the lack of chart or compass. The risks and dangers involved were trivial compared with Abraham's positive assurance of God's presence in and purpose for his life. If he had known where he was going, he might have reached his destination safely, but then again he might never even have begun the journey. Knowledge may indeed be power, as Francis

Bacon held, but there is also in belief power of an incomparable kind.

More than this, belief — which is the work of the mind in faith — holds within itself a promise of greater, better knowledge. Believing is where all knowing must begin. Only as I go forth from what I call myself in trusting relationship to a reality beyond myself, do I gain the perspective and motive for my seeking. One of the deepest truths of faith is that in searching for God I am already found by him, that I could not desire him if I did not already possess him. God alone is the sufficient explanation of our search for God. And so we press on, running the race that is set before us, in the conviction that we shall someday know God even as now we are known by him.

Do you agree that we should distinguish carefully between knowing facts and knowing persons? Or do you think this distinction is overdrawn in the chapter?

How do you understand and respond to the author's emphasis that knowledge of God is more than personal alone?

Consider the act of praying to God as a way of knowing God and being known by him. What sort of knowledge, if any, can prayer give us?

3

"Through Jesus Christ our Lord"

From the preceding chapter it is clear that knowing God is not a one-way process. Instead, it is a mutual recognition in which God himself takes the first and utterly decisive step toward us. We do not have to seek out God entirely on our own, as if God were some sort of Great Fact waiting to be uncovered by man's determined inquiry. Within our very searching we discover God coming toward us, moving graciously and commandingly into the orbit of our experiences. God alone can account for the knowledge human beings have of him. To learn that this is so, and its momentous consequences for all our living, is the assured foundation of genuine, vital faith.

But what is the part played by Jesus Christ in this two-way process of knowing God and being known by him? Shall we think of Christ as being no more than a kind of bridge spanning the extremities between God and man, making possible a contact and communion which would otherwise be impossible to us? Or shall we see in Christ the pioneer of human faith, the advance scout of our way to God? Both views have been taken by thoughtful Christians. While they are by no means untrue, they fall quite short of the essential truth concerning Christ, especially in relation to our knowledge of God.

Christ as the Human Face of God

A more positive and substantial way of putting the Christian truth about Christ must be found. Jesus Christ may be rightly thought of as the human face of God. That is, he carries into life the thrust of God's own being and acting; he expresses as "very man" the fullness of concern and purpose that belong to "very God." Christ represents, because in truth he is, the manward side of God, the presence of God in and among men. Neither a mere point of contact nor a purely human "exhibit A" of saintly genius, Jesus Christ is God's own self-expression and self-giving. In him, God is engaged in reconciling the world to himself. In him the living God acts sovereignly and lovingly for man's eternal good. Thus we see in Christ our best and truest clue to God's mysterious way with us.

Therefore, if the Christian is asked, "How do you know God?" he will answer, "Through Jesus Christ our Lord." These words, with which the public prayers of the church are often concluded, specify the focus of our Christian worship. They tell us where we must look, to whom we must go, if God is to be truly known. He who sees Christ sees God the Father, too. And unless he fixes his attention and allegiance upon Christ, he cannot see the God whom Christ called his Father and ours. Just what this means for understanding and practicing the knowledge of God will concern us in this chapter.

Christ as Word

Christ, we say, is the "revelation" of God. Revelation is a very large, grand word indeed, and it is frequently used without care or preciseness. In the Bible, revelation has the meaning of an unveiling of that which has previously been concealed. In this respect revelation is like every other instance of knowledge which brings into light what before has been in darkness. But when the Bible speaks of revelation it confines this unveiling to the action of God. It is God who breaks out of his own hiddenness, who decides to make himself known and so removes the veil or mask which stands in our way.

The biblical picture of God emphasizes that all revelation is his self-revelation. The God of Abraham, Isaac, and Jacob, of Moses and the prophets is one who does not wait to be found out by man. On the contrary, he makes the first move, sends his Spirit forth from himself in order to declare his will and share his purpose with us. He reaches out and grasps men where he finds them, takes them by surprise, and claims them for his own. This is the characteristic initiative or priority of God which, as we have seen already, is the ultimate source of all our faith in him.

However, it is possible to stress the divine initiative to such an extent that we may lose sight of the very element of revelation itself. Let us not forget that the gospel speaks of God's appearing, taking human shape, becoming visible so that in his light we may see light. Priority does not mean inaccessibility, but presence. What we sing, pray, and preach about in our churches is the message that God has come in person, knowing our life from the inside, and putting himself on a par with us by taking the form of a servant. "God with us" — that is what the word Immanuel means, one of the earliest titles given to Christ. It is also a statement of the Christian gospel in the shortest possible form, as it signifies that God has drawn near and shown himself to us in our own form, on our own ground.

The test of revelation, after all, is simply that it reveals. Unless it brings things formerly dark into the light of day or gives us better vision for seeing things already there, why call it revelation? We do no honor to God's disclosure of himself in Jesus Christ by insisting upon its isolation from all other sorts of meaning, or by refusing to apply to that disclosure those standards of reasonableness which we accept elsewhere. If we try to protect revelation from the "prying eye of reason," we should not be astonished when others suspect that we have something to hide, rather than something to show and give to the world.

Revelation, then, is to be known and judged by the insight and illumination it brings. Its truth is to be measured not merely in terms of sheer impact but of intelligibility. The capacity of the Christian revelation to make sense of our existence should not be underrated or neglected. "Once I was blind, but now I can see" — this testimony is an indispensable fruit of God's revealing activity in Christ. Revelation, let us say, is a miracle of meaning; it can neither be exempt from reasonable interpretation nor be dismissed as wholly unreasonable.

And Jesus Christ, we believe, does bring just this sort of sense or reason into the world as well as into our understanding of it. Christian faith sees in him not the final answer to every question but the significant clue to meaning in every experience. Christ has been able to be the way and the life for man only because he is also the truth. He has challenged minds as well as stirred hearts. In him we find, as centuries of believers have found before us, both depth and breadth of meaning, which stimulates our search for truth even as that search is being satisfied.

It would be a great mistake to suppose that God's revelation in Christ solves all problems magically or automatically. Our decision and obedience in loyalty to Christ are still demanded; we are not excused from running with patience the race that is set before us; and the mystery of life grows, not lessens, with the knowledge we acquire through faith. Yet revelation does place all our problems and puzzlements in what may be called the divine perspective. Instead of providing us with answers in the back of the book, so to speak, God's self-expression in Christ places a whole new value on our questions, giving us the assurance that they are God's questions, too. In faith we do not stop questioning God but we become answerable to him. Indeed, we ourselves are being questioned by him in our confrontation with his Word spoken in Christ.

This Christian name for Christ, the Word of God, indicates that in Christ God has willed to take us into his confidence by making plain his design and strategy for the world's redemption. He does not stand mute when we put our questions of anxious doubt to him; he has spoken and speaks still "through Jesus Christ our Lord." Although God does not provide us with pat, ready-made solutions when he comes to us in Christ, he shows us where we have to look, and that we must keep on looking, if we are to share his promise and vision of a renewed humanity with him. As God's own Word to us about himself, Christ means that we do not have to make our human journey all alone, but are fortified and illumined by the wisdom and counsel of indubitable accents of his voice sounding in the very midst of life.

In ordinary experience, words have many uses. They may simply be signals for behavior, like "Stop" or "Go"; they may be pointers referring to observable facts, like "cheese" or "car"; or they may be terms of value, like "good" or "bad." Some words, of course, have greater reach and significance than others. But all words take their tone and character from the person who speaks them; they communicate the presence of the speaker and open up the possibility of conversation with him.

Thus it is with the Word of God. Jesus Christ is not a word spoken long ago by a speaker who has been silent ever since. He is the manner of God's speaking here and now, not only the what but the how of God's speaking. Our human words fulfill their functions and then die out or are forgotten; but Christ is a living Word, spoken, to be sure, once upon a time in unparalleled depth and clarity, but speaking still as faith responds to his insistent presence. For God is always breaking through to men, even in what seem to be times of anguished silence, so that there is no speech or language in which his voice may not be heard.

Dietrich Bonhoeffer draws an important contrast between word as "address to men" and word as "idea." He shows how these two understandings of the Word of God bear upon our view of Christ. The word as idea is already there, resting in itself, waiting to be listened to and understood. But the word as address is an event which happens between two living beings; it occurs only in community, and it requires a reply. Much of our thinking about Christ, says Bonhoeffer, is spoiled by the notion that he is a timeless truth or idea, like those of mathematics or philosophy. What we must realize, he goes on, is that Christ is God addressing himself to us, creating fellowship with him.

Such a dynamic understanding of the Word of God as Bonhoeffer suggests is sorely needed in the Christian enterprise today. Our religion, it seems, is very largely talk — talk about God, about Christ, about the church, about faith. Yet how seldom it becomes listening to and hearing what God has to say to us! It is almost as if we were afraid to let God get his Word in, so preoccupied are we with saying kind words on his behalf. To such a wordy generation as ours comes the reminder from the Bible, "Be still, and know that I am God."

Such knowledge may emerge out of many experiences and approach us through many channels, yet it is Christ as God's Word who guarantees that it is true. God reveals himself in any way he chooses, but he has chosen to reveal himself in his own Word. As Bonhoeffer writes, God has bound himself to the Word so as to speak it to men, and he does not go back on his Word. By his choice of Jesus Christ as Word, God gives us plain and powerful assurance of his self-revealing love.

Christ as Lord

As the Word or self-expression of God, Christ is also the Lord of man. These two terms, when taken together, probably catch up as well as any other titles the practical, lived meaning of Christ for Christians. As Word emphasizes his relation, unique and singular, to God, so Lord points toward

41

his universal relationship to mankind. Yet we would be mistaken if we thought that the first of these terms indicated Christ's divinity while the second designates his humanity. It is as God that Christ is related to man, and it is as man that he is related to God; otherwise there would be no relation to describe.

Lordship signifies rightful authority, which is not a very popular idea at the present time. The days are long past when some persons were regarded as having intrinsic and personal superiority over others which justified their right to power. Today we think of authority as accidental — arising from favorable circumstances — and functional — coming about as the result of executive responsibility, a way of getting a job done. "Lord" is still a courtesy title used in referring to certain members of the British nobility, and that is just about its only use outside the religious sphere. In our present world, rightful personal authority is at best a difficult and old-fashioned idea.

Why, then, should we retain and underline this title in our thought of Jesus Christ? Is anything more involved here than being faithful to a biblical and churchly tradition of long standing? Can "Lord" actually say what needs saying? Let us see.

Jesus of Nazareth, called the Christ (or "Messiah" in Hebrew), is one man among many; he is not a divine apparition or "idea." As "very man" he knows what we are made of, what we have to face, the possibilities that lie open to us; he is one of us, not some strange intruder from another world than this. A fully and individually human being, not "man-in-general" nor half-man and half-God, Jesus Christ lives out his life and dies his death as each of us must also do. He knows the inner meaning of work, love, suffering, joy. He struggles with temptation, faces loneliness and hostility, enjoys companionship and a measure of momentary success. The heights and depths of our existence are matters of personal experience to him. He is not less a man, but more, than any of us can ever be.

Did Jesus know that he was God's Messiah, appointed for the saving of the whole world? Biblical scholars are of different minds on this point. Whether he himself was conscious of his place in God's plan or not, his followers soon made this identification. Hence it is impossible, even in the earliest biblical records, to separate what Jesus thought about himself from what the disciples believed him to be. The "Jesus of history" is inseparable from the "Christ of faith." What matters most, however, is that an actual, historical person is seen by faith to be worthy of supreme devotion. The man Christ Jesus thus becomes the new center of man's profoundest yearnings and most earnest expectations.

The first confession of faith in the Christian church is the glad cry, "Jesus is Lord." Brief as it is, it holds a wealth of meaning; on the lips of a community nurtured in the Jewish Scriptures, it declares that God's long search for man has reached its climax, come to fulfillment, in a life of mysterious might and grace. That life had shown forth, for all the world to see, the wisdom and power of the most high God, conquering sin and even death and opening up the way of reconciliation through suffering, yet finally triumphant love. God in that life had come home to man in order to bring man home to him.

Since this had happened concretely, unmistakably, within the man Christ Jesus, the early church had been called and gathered out of many tongues and races, as the story of Pentecost told in the book of Acts said. Here was a new way of being in the world, a new community stirred by a new hope. No longer did men need to bear the burden of their own guilt in self-centered anguish and despair; no longer did they have to strain themselves toward a perfection they did not possess. God in Christ had taken on himself the awful cost of man's estrangement in sin, and had freely bestowed on men the only righteousness that really counted — that of grace through faith in God's redeeming Word.

What was made everlastingly plain in Christ was that the tragic grip of sin and death on man had actually been broken once for all, so that by becoming part of God's work in him men could find their true and whole selves again in genuine freedom. Yes, the Christian faith began as a victory celebration, founded on the fact that, in the glowing words of St. Augustine, "[Christ] our life descended hither and took away our death, and killed him [death], out of the abundance of his own life." A humble man had been conceived and born, had suffered, taught, healed, and died; but then this same man had risen, ascended to God, and been given kingly power over all things in heaven and on earth. Small wonder therefore that he should be called Lord.

So it is Christ's victory, won by virtue of obedience to his mission as the Word of God, that gives him his rightful authority as Lord of man. That authority is all the more real because it has been earned, hard-won, wrought out of the very fabric and stuff of the life we know as our own. Christ did not take the world by storm like a conquering hero. He identified himself with us in such a way that the majesty of God stands revealed in his very meekness, as it could not be in the exertion of sheer power and compelling force. Christ humbled himself, and "therefore," as Scripture says, God has highly exalted him. He does not wear his authority as a kind of badge that everyone can see and must respect. Instead, he wins our final allegiance simply by being what he is — ". . . the right man on our side, the man of God's own choosing," in the words of Luther's great hymn.

Of course this authority is only visible to the eyes of faith. But this does not mean that it is our faith which makes him Lord. Rather, it is his Lordship that creates, sustains, and increases our faith. Since God in Christ has found his human voice and face, the old illusion of distance has been overcome by "the Beyond that is within." True, not everyone acknowledges that this has happened. That is because the signs of God's appearing can be read in many ways, and faith is only one way of interpreting them. Men are as free to choose or reject God's love as they were before Christ came. For love always respects another's freedom; even more, love invites participation and does not demand conformity or compliance. A loving God gives what he asks and makes humanly possible what he proclaims. In Christ, our faith affirms, God has done just that.

Christ as Mediator

Through Christ, God speaks and acts forgivingly and savingly; and again, through Christ, we men dare to belong in faith to "love's redeeming work." One of the oldest and most spacious words in all the Christian vocabulary expresses this quality of thoroughness — the word "Mediator." Until we find a better word to say what we have gratefully discerned and valued most in Christ, this one will have to do. But like so many other faith words, this too has gotten secularized to the point where one wonders if it can still carry its original meaning, and the difficulty should be faced.

A mediator in a labor-management dispute, for example, is a third party, standing between the two conflicting interests, who has the confidence of both precisely because he stands above the battle. He has personally nothing to lose or win either way, and so he can be trusted to be impartial, fair, and even disinterested. Furthermore, what such a mediator can achieve is very likely to be a compromise, a nicely balanced outcome which brings with it neither complete victory nor complete defeat for either of the sides involved.

This understanding of what a mediator is does not help us much when it comes to Jesus Christ. To keep on with our contemporary analogy, it is as if management itself came to labor at the conference table and gave without reserve or subterfuge everything that was being demanded and more besides. Far from being disinterested and impartial, such an act of mediation would be intensely, personally concerned. While the result sought would not be unjust to either party, simple justice would not be the goal, but rather the realizing of a common, all-embracing good. Past wrongs would be gladly and generously forgiven; the resources of one party would be made freely available to the needs of the other; and instead of a bargaining procedure there would be a loving dialogue intent upon establishing a completely new relationship.

If all this seems far-fetched and unheard-of when applied to the ways in which men try to get what they want from each other, it is nevertheless true of what the Christian faith believes to be God's way with man in Christ. God does not send a neutral arbitrator to effect his reconciliation with us; he sends his only-begotten Son instead. Like the rich owner in Jesus' own parable, God takes the terrible risk that he will be misunderstood, that his mediating deed may be rejected and his forgiveness only resented; his Son may even be killed by those to whom he comes in all innocence and candor. Yet the risk does not deter God; he leaves his pride at home and knows no fear as he comes open-handed, seeking only friendship and fellowship with mankind turned away from him in sin. And out of what the world calls tragic defeat, God wrests his strange, ultimate triumph — not over man but for him.

That is the sort of mediation which God offers us in Jesus Christ. Imperfect as our analogy is when compared with the fullness of God's self-expression in the event which Christians believe to be the turning-point of all history, it still can serve to indicate something altogether central in the words "through Jesus Christ our Lord." Putting the matter in human terms, God is the wronged party from whom we have alienated ourselves in sinful self-love. Yet he does not stand aloof, waiting to be shown that we deserve forgiveness or are worthy of his mercy. In Jesus Christ he runs toward us undisguised and unprotected, offering us his own whole kingdom of peaceable and blessed fellowship. Thus he fulfills his ancient promise to be our God, to make us his people. Here in Christ is a mediator who does not bargain or compromise but who simply and utterly breaks down all barriers and opens the way for God, and to God, in the very heart of man.

Suppose that we who profess and call ourselves Christians were to take this good news with the joyous seriousness that it deserves. Suppose that its glad and liberating truth were not only heard but lived. And suppose that a world which has formed the habit of looking everywhere but to Christ for its salvation were to be led by our faithfulness to turn to him as its true Lord. It may seem fantastic even to think of it. Yet all things, we are told, are possible to God and to men with God. If something like this were to happen in God's good time and by his grace, then the age-old prophecy would indeed become true: "The earth will be filled with the knowledge of God, as the waters cover the sea."

Of all the titles mentioned in the chapter, which one do you yourself find most meaningful in speaking of Christ, and why?

What authority can a Word spoken by God almost two thousand years ago still have for us today?

How, in your own brief statement, would you make clear the meaning of "being a Christian"?

Do you believe that Christ is Lord of the whole world, or only of the Christian church? Explain.

4

The Bible– record of revelation

No one in our day needs to be told how important records are. Every college, hospital, or factory thrives on them, for records are indispensable to their operation. We could hardly say that the chief business of these enterprises is that of producing records, but without the collecting and storing of data they would be helpless in carrying on their work. And while no student, patient, or employee likes to think of himself as being no more than a folder in a file, his best interests are furthered by the keeping of such records. A record is not the real thing, but for all that, it is useful and necessary in gaining an accurate impression of the real.

Take biography, for instance. Biographers tell us of the importance of picking up and following the "paper trail" left by the subject of their work. Birth certificate, work contract, correspondence, will, and death certificate must all be located and scrutinized. There may be photographs, reviews, published or performed works, reminiscences or estimates by other persons to be studied as well. All this mass of records must be carefully weighed and pondered; it may not all be of equal worth in revealing the subject, to be sure, but one never knows just where a bright clue may turn up.

The Bible likewise is a record, or rather a whole vast

complex of records, of many and very different kinds. That is, Scripture consists of documents thrown up in a long history — poems, prayers, chronicles at first or second hand, codes of behavior, visions, sermons, cherished sayings, inventories, accounts of battles, short stories, ancestral records, symbolic narratives, and much else besides. As it stands, between book covers and provided with a table of contents and numbered verses and chapters, it may seem a more unified record than it actually is. We need to be reminded that the material in it comes from periods stretching over more than a thousand years, that it is written in a great variety of styles and for a wide range of purposes, and that the way from Genesis to Revelation is a long, often broken, and meandering path.

A Matter of Record

What is recorded in the Bible? Plainly, it has to do from first to last with one who is variously called Jehovah, Lord of Hosts, the Holy One of Israel, Judge, King, Shepherd, Father — but whom it is not difficult to recognize as God. God is the thread which ties these many books together; they record his deeds, promises, warnings, punishments, rewards; they document his dealings with a people who believed they had been chosen as his own, but who did not always keep faith with him and had to be recalled to obedience and reverence, not once but many times. On every page of Scripture God is somehow made present, whether in public, historic events such as victory or defeat in battle, or in intimate glimpses of persons in their secret selves, like Elijah cowering in his cave. The human pattern of the Bible shifts and changes, but the reference to God is constant and unmistakable.

God is the Subject of the Bible, not in the sense that all its books are written about him, but in the sense that his being and acting are never absent from the tangled web of human events described there. It is the same, too, with the events of nature that enter into the scope of biblical writing; the long and short rhythms of natural change, growth, decay, as well as catastrophe and miracle, are all seen as the mighty acts of God. It is he, as the song puts it, who has the whole world in his hands. He creates, preserves, directs, and consummates its vast processes. He watches over his particular people but shows them no favoritism, as he shapes and teaches Israel for her participation in his universal work. Nothing is too small to escape his notice, and nothing too great to proceed contrary to his purposes. All this and more is what it means to say that God is the Subject of the Bible.

Scripture, then, is the record of revelation, that is, of God's unceasing self-disclosure in the movements and patterns of man's life in the world. But Scripture is not that revelation itself. Its books are written by men and show the marks of human frailty, immaturity, and ignorance as well as those of human insight, courage, and achievement. The Bible is a record of much else besides revelation; it chronicles unsparingly man's lust and longing, grief and unhappiness, fear and faith. This remains true even when God is the evident Subject; for he is described in very human terms as having both positive and negative feelings, a will not unlike our own, and a heart which can be moved to pity or anger.

It is easy for the reader of the Bible to become discouraged and even repelled by all this humanizing of God in its pages, and yet we must ask how otherwise he could be known as the living God. Is it not far better to have this human record as it stands with all its freight of confused thinking, uncertain faith, or outdated imagining, than merely to wish for some other supposedly purer and more accurate record? That in the nature of the case simply cannot be had. We should rather rejoice in the fact that the Bible, with all its traces of human weakness, does make God's self-revelation a matter of record. We may have this treasure in very earthen vessels indeed, but we really do have it. After all, that is the utterly significant point.

The Bible is perhaps too well known, but in another sense it is not known well enough. Familiarity with it, as expressed in our conventional names like "The Good Book" or "Holy Writ," has evidently gotten in the way of a direct and lively apprehension of its contents. How difficult it seems to be for us to come to the reading of Scripture afresh, entering the doors of the biblical world, letting ourselves be stirred or surprised by what we find there, allowing God to speak to us as he spoke to its writers! By placing the Bible high on the shelf of our reverence we have perhaps rendered it safe and innocuous; we may even have weakened its impact and dulled its insights, though of course with the best Christian intentions in the world. In the face of this tendency to idolize and so to sterilize the Bible, it must simply be declared that the whole process should be questioned and stopped.

But we were saying that the Bible makes God's revelation of himself a matter of record. That is Scripture's mighty virtue and chief claim upon our faith. "In the year that king Uzziah died I saw the Lord . . ."; "the Word of the Lord came to me . . ."; "I know in whom I have believed . . ." — these are but illustrations of a quality of direct, indubitable experience which is manifest throughout the Bible and gives to it the firsthand character we mentioned in the first chapter of this book. The men and women of the Bible were those who had been caught and grasped in the press of everyday circumstances by one whom they had to recognize as the true and only God. They saw "the works of his hands" in wind and weather, the rise and fall of kingdoms and dynasties, and the intimate details of marriage and family life. Homely incidents and grand public events alike proclaimed the ever-active, ever-watchful, living God. The Bible, therefore, is a record of the Lord Almighty as encountered and responded to by people very like ourselves.

51

We would however be mistaken if we thought of Scripture as being the record of separate and distinct experiences only. What runs through it is the sense that God is consistent with himself, that he can always be trusted even in adverse circumstances because of his faithfulness or steadfastness. In him there is "no variableness, neither shadow or turning." That is because he has given men signs by which he may be known and marks by which his presence and power may be detected in the ordinary run of things. He has established his covenant with men, has bound himself to men, in such a way that they and he belong to one another for all eternity. That covenant, signaled in the rainbow to Noah after the flood, has been again and again renewed in spite of men's repeated failures to live up to it. Thus God has shown himself to be, from man's point of view, wholly reliable and dependable; his ways may not be our ways nor his thoughts our thoughts, but his mercy is everlasting and his teaching is sure.

What we have then in the Bible is a clearly human record of a more-than-human encounter. What we do not have is a divinely dictated manuscript or a completely unflawed, infallible document that guarantees its own authenticity and is altogether above criticism. But this is not to call into question the Bible's incomparable worth and truth as a book arising from and addressed to human faith. Neither is it to deny that God's self-revealing does occur in Scripture in a life-changing way, as it did for men like Augustine or Wesley, William Booth, or Toyohiko Kagawa. Still less can we deny that in the last analysis it takes God to account for the writing of the books of the Bible. Only inspiration — that is, the incoming of the Holy Spirit — can explain this kind of writing with its sureness of touch in handling the things of God. Again and again, the Bible has given proof that it is not simply a record of something happening to someone else at another time. It also invites us to take part in the events which it describes "through faith."

Christ in the Bible

In the preceding chapter we considered what it means to call Jesus Christ the Word of God. But this same phrase is often used of Scripture, too. Men claim to have found God speaking to them in the Bible just as in the person and work of Christ. Indeed, it has usually been through the medium of Scripture that God's voice speaking in Christ has been heard most clearly. This powerful and undeniable connection between Christ and the Bible is one which we must try to fathom and rely on, if we are to come to know the living God.

First of all, the Bible as a whole claims our Christian attention and understanding. What we call the Old Testament belongs to our faith just as much as the New Testament does. The fact that we share the Old Testament with Judaism is highly significant; it points to a common heritage and source of faith for both Jew and Christian. We too, as the apostle Paul was fond of saying, are the children of Abraham. The same God who led Moses and his people through the wilderness of Canaan directs the lives of Christians in the world today. The psalms traditionally ascribed to King David are still the spiritual food and drink of our own worship. In these and other ways it is made abundantly clear that the whole Bible, not some parts of it, belongs by right to Christian faith.

Yet there is a tremendous difference between Jewish and Christian modes of reading and viewing the Old Testament. That difference obviously comes from the central, utterly crucial place given to Jesus Christ in our own faith. For Christ is the Messiah, God's Anointed, long awaited and predicted in the religion of the Jews. He has come in the fullness of time; the ancient haunting dream has at last been realized; the old longings have been satisfied in him. As it is written in the Letter to the Hebrews in our New Testament, "In many and various ways God spoke of old to our fathers by the prophets; but in these last days he has spoken to us by a Son" (Hebrews 1:1-2). While Judaism still looks ahead, Christianity looks back to the point in history where God finally broke through and dwelt with us in Christ. The difference, therefore, is between expectation and fulfillment, prediction and announcement, waiting and arrival.

Some Christians in the early church were so impressed by this difference that they tried to separate completely the Jewish Scriptures from the revelation given in Christ. They even denied that it was the same God who spoke to men in the two Testaments. The New Testament, they felt, had annulled forever the force of the Old. A God of love and mercy such as Christ proclaimed could in their view have little if anything to do with a God of justice and wrath as described in Jewish faith. And so they drew a sharp line between the two Testaments, claiming that Christians must stand on only one side and make up their minds once for all to leave behind their Jewish heritage.

The reason why we must not take this course, however, is a simple and important one. Jesus himself said that he came "not to destroy but to fulfill." In other words, the truth that he is the expected Messiah makes faith in him continuous with the faith of the Jewish past, and not a completely different kind of faith. To be sure, it also judges Jewish faith as something preparatory and incomplete as it stands, but not as wholly false or vain. Those Jewish Christians in the early church who thought that entry into the new faith must be by means of such ancient Jewish practices as circumcision or keeping the dietary laws were wrong, of course. A Christian does not need to do over again what Christ has done for us all — namely, abolishing the wall of hostility which man's own sin had created between himself and God, thus replacing fear with confidence and the old striving after righteousness with a new and grateful awareness of God's costly and precious love. This is good news indeed, and yet the goodness and newness of the gospel can be known only by those who have learned well what God was teaching mankind in the Jewish Scriptures: that he is not a God to be trifled with but is truly our Creator, Governor, and Redeemer who has made us restless for himself, and calls us to be his own people and to do his will.

As with his disciples following the resurrection, so to us as well Christ opens the Scriptures — all the Scriptures — by the power and wisdom of God that speak savingly to us in him. The record of God's self-revelation, from beginning to end, is centered in Christ. Now everything in that record comes to focus, becomes one, and is illuminated with new light. This is the second point of great significance in our Christian reading of the Bible. It may be put like this: the Word spoken in Christ is witnessed to and echoed in the words of Scripture, so that we possess in them a sure and valid clue to what God has all along been saying. Or rather, we find such a clue in the greater Word that gives its meaning to the lesser ones, shining through them, as it were, without either destroying or lessening them.

Our ancestors, of course, carried this point pretty far when they regarded everything in the Old Testament as foreshadowing the New, even supposing that a love-poem like the Song of Solomon really meant to declare Christ's love for his church, to take but one example. Nevertheless, they were right in emphasizing that a Christian necessarily reads the Bible backward and forward from Christ, who is the keyword or password which orders and gives value to the whole.

Where the viewer stands determines what he sees. The view of Fujiyama seen from Lake Hakone in Japan is serenely beautiful, but the same mountain glimpsed from an airplane on flight from Tokyo to Hong Kong has a different sort of beauty. Our view of Scripture, similarly, is determined by what Paul delighted to call the mind of Christ. We stand in faith at the point where God has uttered his own Word, and hence all the words spoken about God or on his behalf by men take on new meaning. That meaning is not narrowed but deepened and broadened as we follow out the clue to Scripture provided by the mind of Christ.

How shall we define that clue? Surely, once again, it is the theme which recurs so often in the Bible, of a loving God who will not let us go but cares mightily and graciously for us, who delights to give himself to us and only asks that we take him at his Word. Since Jesus Christ is the very embodiment of God's love, he represents the climax of all revelation and the key to an understanding of the record of that revelation set down in the Bible. In his light we see light. In him as Word of God and Lord of man all things cohere, fit together, make sense.

The Bible therefore becomes God's Word when Christ is there disclosed and responded to in faith. Centuries of Christian reading of the Scriptures have abundantly demonstrated their capacity to do exactly that, and each of us in his own turn may make the same tremendous discovery.

The Bible and Tradition

One of the most perplexing problems about the Bible is its relationship to what our Roman Catholic neighbors call tradition. Just what this problem is may be made clearer by an illustration. The Constitution of the United States is a document which anyone can read who takes the trouble to secure a copy. It is authoritative for the processes of our government, the test of the rightness or wrongness of proposed laws, and the basis of our freedom and responsibility as citizens. However, the meaning of the Constitution is not something which is simple and self-evident; it can only be grasped as it comes to us through national history itself; executive actions, legislative debates, and court decisions are all required fully to understand its meaning.

Similarly, the Bible does not stand completely alone but has entered into the life and faith of the Christian church so deeply that almost every prayer, every hymn, every sermon has what may be called a biblical element. Hence we do not approach the Bible as a single reader takes up a published volume. We come to Scripture through the ways in which it has been traditionalized — that is, interpreted, used, and appealed to within the community of faith.

This fact is of the greatest importance, as it indicates that there is no purely individual avenue to Scripture as a ready-made standard of conduct and belief. Again, where the reader stands determines what sort of meaning he will find. Some look to the Bible to justify one doctrine or practice, some another. Scripture has been used to defend infant baptism and to attack it, to authorize bishops and to prohibit them, and so on. Whatever may be said about the Bible as the final norm of Christian judgment and behavior, the fact is that it can be, and has been, taken in many different and contrary ways.

The situation is even more complex than this. If we suppose that Scripture is the original form of faith to which all our traditions must be subject, then we must face the actual historical truth that Scripture is the result of the traditionalizing process — sayings of Jesus remembered and relayed from one generation to the next, acts of prayer and worship which find their way into the written record, interpretations of the meaning of Christ designed to correct misunderstanding or to persuade a pagan environment, and much else in the same vein. Yes, the Bible itself is a crystallizing of traditions which grew up within the Christian community; it cannot therefore be deemed superior to all tradition on the ground that it presents the pure state of the gospel as it was before human error had done its devastating work.

Today, in the deepening dialogue that is taking place between Roman Catholics and Protestants, the issue of

Scripture and tradition has a prominent place. Two things are becoming increasingly plain in this conversation. The first is that neither tradition nor Scripture can claim to be the sole standard of church belief and practice. The other is that both Scripture and tradition enter into the faith by which we are nurtured and sustained. Since we cannot do without either, we must learn to live effectively with both. Protestants should be willing to see and grant more generously the force of tradition in the making and use of the Bible; Roman Catholics should be ready to accept the Bible as the testing-ground of their traditional doctrine and devotion.

All this is really part of a larger matter, that of the church in its unceasing intercourse with the Bible. Whenever there has been renewal or reformation in the church, the Bible has been rediscovered as the book of life. As we have seen, this is because the Bible witnesses to what God has done for us in Jesus Christ, and witnesses in an incomparable way. For all the tradition involved in the formation of the Bible, it still stands closer to the events recorded in its pages than any of our present churches ever can. Although it is impossible to ignore the intervening centuries as if they never existed, it is imperative to look in faith back toward the time and place in which our faith arose and took its original shape. Only so can we know, or rightly proclaim, him who is Lord of man and Word of God.

The Bible and the Holy Spirit

Yet it would be quite wrong to regard the Bible only as a volume of retrospection or recall. If we are in earnest about hearing God speak, what we shall hear is the living voice of his present will. As members of the church of Christ we have more to do than to congratulate ourselves on being the descendants of our ancestors. Faith languishes and dies when it becomes purely imitative or repetitive. In turning to the Bible we find far more than a storehouse of ancient wisdom to be recited and held fast; we are drawn into a living dialogue with God in company with prophets and apostles, saints and martyrs of past ages.

For the Bible is a book of surprises. We never know just when or where the living God may break through and speak to us; as Coleridge wrote, the Bible "finds us where we live." Many small groups formed for Bible reading and study have been learning that this is indeed so. The experience of coming to terms with God as he speaks through Scripture may be dangerous to my self-esteem or upsetting to my well-established notions of religion. It may launch me on untried, costly paths of service, teaching me as if for the first time who my neighbor really is. It may not so much confirm what I think I know already about God as it may require me to change my mind and habits as a church member. It may give a wholly unexpected meaning to my everyday experiences.

In other words, we have to reckon with the Spirit in our reading of the Bible. Without the presence of the Holy Spirit, the church would constantly be tempted to regard the Bible as a closed book. But with the presence of the Holy Spirit it is anything but that. We do not have in our possession a collection of ready-made truths demanding our unquestioning acceptance. Instead we have the permanent possibility of a dialogue with the God who lives and speaks, not out of some remote past but in the here-and-now of his Spirit's visitation. Sometimes we are inclined to think of the Holy Spirit, following the Gospel of John to be sure, as the Comforter sent to console and compensate us for the absence of Christ. It is wiser and truer to think of the Holy Spirit as the Interpreter who leads us by the path of Scripture to the very presence of Christ "in the midst." God's gift of his Spirit to the church means that Christ himself is our eternal contemporary.

And by the same token the gift of God's Spirit to the church means that the Bible does not consist of regulations for righteousness which have to be brought up to date from time to time. The Bible is not a rule book but a guidebook; its meaning and bearing upon our life in the world depends upon the presence of the Spirit who leads us into all truth. "Where the Spirit of the Lord is, there is freedom" (2 Corinthians 3:17). God's love for us is such that he not only makes available a record of his revelation, but also sends us his Spirit as "the truth teaching within." Thus he opens up for us a future in which more truth will yet break forth from his Word, in which his redeeming love will more and more be set free from the pages of the Bible to do God's work within us and among us.

What significant differences do you see between the view that the Bible is the record of revelation, and the view that it is revelation itself?

Is there one central clue for understanding the Bible, especially where passages seem confusing or contradictory to each other? If you think so, what is it?

Do you think the author makes too much of human tradition in the formation of Scripture? How would you express the role of tradition in our use of the Bible in the church today?

What is your response to the remark that the Bible is a guidebook, not a rule book? Would you prefer to say it differently? If so, how?

5

The church– its mystery and meaning

Today a great many people are talking excitedly about the church. They belabor it for its obvious shortcomings, question its ability to stand up under rapid social change, and worry over its future in our secular culture. Like the woman who was brought to Jesus for healing, the church has indeed "suffered much at the hands of many doctors." What is amazing nowadays is that the church can survive so many premature reports of its death. It may not change as readily or move as quickly as perhaps it should, but it has demonstrated a remarkable power to outlive its severest critics before, and will very likely do so again.

Most of the talk that is concerned with the present difficulties and the future destiny of the church goes on within the practical sphere. We are asking how this human institution can improve itself by altering its structures or rethinking its functions, just as a business firm might decide to take stock of its assets and liabilities. There can be no doubt that on this practical level much can and should be done to fit the church better for its mission in and for the world.

But when we ask why the church continues to outlast criticism and adversity we are on a different, deeper level. What is the secret of the church's vitality? There must be something here beyond the visible surface, something more meaningful and more mysterious than membership statistics, organizations, or programs, something we cannot contrive but only discover and express. Let us think together, then, about the mystery and the meaning of the Christian church.

Visible and Invisible

The church's reality is greater than the forms in which it appears at any time or place. No human institution can fully express that reality, and yet the church cannot be real at all unless it becomes actual in the worship, witness, and service of men and women like ourselves. We have the treasure of the church's life and faith, as Paul wrote, in very human, earthen vessels. It is often hard for us to recognize that the vessels are not the treasure; it is equally difficult to see that the treasure is really contained, though never confined, within the vessels. But we should make a resolute attempt to do both of these things. When we criticize the church for failure to act in a certain way, we are insisting that its true nature should come through more clearly into its visible structuring and functioning. And when we declare that, despite its many faults, the church is nevertheless set down in the world as the bodying-forth of God's purpose for mankind, we see truly that it has an invisible dimension which cannot be denied. The treasure needs to be conveyed in the vessels if it is not to be entirely lost. The vessels need to be made fit and worthy to hold the treasure, if they are not going to become irrelevant or meaningless.

So let us beware of trying to give over-simple answers to complex questions. In our impatience to improve our churches let us not forget that they do carry more or less effectively the gospel into a bewildering and suffering world. But in our confidence that God has chosen such vessels as these to advance his work, let us not fool ourselves about the actual flaws and liabilities which are apparent on every hand.

The idea that something invisible can also be real may strike some of us as very odd indeed. In an earlier chapter it was pointed out how very fact-minded people of our time are, and how difficult it is for what cannot be known through the senses to establish any sort of claim as truth. In our assertion that "seeing is believing" we are likely to be unaware that believing may also be a kind of seeing. What is seen, after all, does not need to be believed. It is simply there to be noticed. But there are many things by which we take our bearings and find life-direction — things which lie below, or possibly above, the level of common sense and practicality, such as moral principles or personal attachments, hopes, or ideals for a better world. I believe in justice for my fellowman even though what I see around me is the very opposite. Yet I do not give up my belief, but allow it to shape my conduct and motivate my choices. It is the same in other fields of endeavor and concern; what we believe or trust in enables us to see beyond the everyday visibilities, and so to make the invisible real.

Think of the church, then, as being invisible in a similar way. It belongs to the realm of motivation, loyalty, goals, and principles for life. Not its distance from the things that matter most to people, but its intimate connection with them, marks the church's invisible reality. Some things lie too close, not too far away, to be easily or clearly seen; and the church is one of them.

How often in the Bible faith is pictured as having to do with what is invisible! It is called "the evidence of things not seen," and a man of faith is commended for having "endured as seeing him who is invisible." Let us admit that the range of the visible was not so large in biblical times as in our own, so that much of what was then unseen may be seen today. And yet the fine paradox remains. Seeing the unseen is the very business of faith, and also of the love and hope bound up with faith. The church, insofar as it can make a home for these three "Christian virtues" in the needy heart of man, keeps alive the presence of the invisible in close and inner contact with what is visible. We cannot live by what is seen alone but must, in order to be human, keep touch with those unseen realities that beckon and guide and will not let us rest.

When our ancestors spoke of the "church invisible," they also had in mind the community of the living with the dead in the household of faith. They viewed the history of the church as a long and shining procession of prophets and apostles, saints and martyrs who "being dead, yet speak" to men and women in the present. By this invisible society of those Christians who have gone on before us, we are surrounded, sustained, and encouraged for our own witnessing and serving. Some of our most cherished hymns voice this note of grateful awareness that we do not stand alone in living out our faith, but may rely upon the inspiring example and assured presence of those "loved long since but lost awhile."

There is still another way of stating that the church is more than meets the eye. St. Augustine has written eloquently of the "two cities," the heavenly and the earthly, which are built upon two opposing principles — love of God and love of self. He pointed out that the church moves between both poles, since it is both divinely purposed and humanly conditioned. Yet insofar as the church remains obedient to its heavenly vision it bodies forth in time and space the work and plan of God who is himself invisible. The church exists on both the heavenly and earthly levels, but there can be no question as to where its heart ought to be and its loyalty belongs.

These illustrations from the past may be supplemented from the present. When a young person is ordained to the ministry today, he or she is ordained to the whole church of Christ, not to one particular church. The ordinances, or sacraments, of baptism and the Lord's Supper, while administered in various ways by different denominations, nevertheless express important meanings of our "citizenship in heaven," as Augustine would have called it. That is, although congregations or denominations carry on the work of initiation, ordination, or celebration, they do it as trustees or stewards of the greater church they represent. But where is this whole church of Jesus Christ to be found? It cannot be the mere adding up of all particular churches because it gives to them whatever truth or worth they may possess. It is as if our separate churches all were broken lights of a universal radiance, or diverging paths which could be followed back to a common Lord who is "the pioneer and perfecter of our faith." Here again the visible runs out into the invisible, and the greater church gives meaning to the lesser churches which the eye of man can see.

What we most need in the churches of today is new eyes for invisibles, and especially for that church unseen, but very real, which ought to guide and support our efforts in sharing the gospel with the world. Such a vision can save us both from despair of doing any good at all and from complacency in thinking more highly of ourselves than we have any right to think. Yes, our churches are not the church, but they are what we have of the church, and they draw whatever faith or life is in them from the spirit of our unseen Lord.

Sustained in Worship

One of the ways in which this visible-invisible character of the church comes home to us most often, and most directly, is that of "sacramental" worship. Today members of some so-called "free churches" tend to think of worship as chiefly a preaching service, to which may be added on occasion the celebration of the ordinances or sacraments. Hence it is important to recognize that, from the beginning, Christian worship has centered in the corporate action of the Lord's Supper, and membership in the church has been marked by a baptismal rite. These events are not to be "tacked on" to worship, but they are essential to the meaning and practice of worship offered in the name of Christ.

In the early years of the church's history all worship was sacramental worship. A common meal or "love feast" called *agape* was held each week for those already committed to Christ as members one of another in the church. Somewhat later, this meal was supplemented by readings from Scripture interpreted through preaching, and by prayers. Soon the full service for the Lord's day consisted of a preparatory stage giving instruction to those who were looking forward to church membership, the catechumens; and a second stage for members only in which the Lord's Supper was the climax, called the "mass of the faithful."

Therefore the sacramental element in Christian worship is the older and many of us would say the truer part in the church's regular and public services. But what do we mean by calling worship sacramental? The very word has become unfamiliar and even suspect in some quarters, because it suggests a Catholic rather than a Protestant understanding of worship. Nevertheless, we are all being forced by the ecumenical movement to rethink many things, including the ordinances or sacraments and their place in the worship of God.

There is a standard definition of a sacrament which goes back to the Middle Ages but has truth for us still. It is this: "A sacrament is an outward and visible sign of an inward and spiritual grace." What comes at once to mind when these words are read? Perhaps such symbols as a wedding ring or a birthday cake, which express outwardly and visibly our inner feelings toward each other. It is all too easy to confuse the meaning of a sacrament with such human signs of fidelity between husband and wife or solidarity in the family. But that is not what the

THE CHURCH—ITS MYSTERY AND MEANING

definition says. Instead it points to the action of God (or "grace") in expressing his concern for men and women like ourselves, and within the familiar world of food and drink and cleansing water at that.

A sacrament, then (and surely this is also true of an ordinance), is an outward and visible sign that God visits and enlivens us by his Spirit, through the "means of grace" used and blessed by his Son. To be sure, it is a sign and not the reality signified; but it is not on that account a mere label or pointer. A sacrament, or an ordinance, is something done by members of a church which reenacts what God has done for us in Christ. It is a parable in action, "the most active form of faith," a student called it.

The sacrament, or ordinance, of the Supper, called also Communion, Mass, or Eucharist, has taken on a host of meanings in the long course of Christian experience. For some, it is chiefly a memorial service in which we remember Jesus and pattern our actions after his own in the upper room the night before his death. For others, it is observed as an experience of fellowship or communion with the risen Lord whereby their mutual love is deepened and greatened in the church. Still others emphasize the aspect of thanksgiving, suggested by the Greek word *eucharistia*, and find in it an occasion for Christian celebration, joyously grateful for God's incomparable gift of Christ.

Now all these meanings are the birthright of every Christian, and no one of them can stand alone without the others in the worship of the church. The meaning of remembrance is basic to the others, for did not our Lord himself say, "Do this in remembrance of me"? We look back in time to that event in which the last supper of Jesus with his disciples became the first supper or lovefeast of the Christian church. We recall his words on that occasion and repeat his own actions as recorded in the New Testament.

Yet if the Lord's Supper were no more than a memorial

service, it could never have had the central importance for worship which generations of Christians have seen in it. We do not deny this basic meaning when we say, as we must, that it is not a dead Jesus but the living Christ who calls us together to worship in his name. "Where two or three are gathered together," as he himself promised, "there am I in the midst." Thus it is presence, the "real presence" if you will, which gives the Supper its momentous truth and worth as an act of faith. We are one with each other because we are one in him. Our fellowship in the church cuts sharply across the human lines of separation or distinction — national, racial, geographical, or creedal. That is because Jesus Christ himself embodied the love of God which knows no human bounds and overleaps all man-made barriers. A mystical writer once put this well by declaring that we Christians are like the spokes of a wheel: the nearer we come to the center, the closer we are to each other. And that is surely true of the great sacrament or ordinance of "life together" that we call Communion.

The third meaning, grateful celebration, is perhaps most often absent from our services today, especially in Protestantism. We therefore need to give particular stress to it. A modern poet asks, "Why, when you talk of God, do your eyes narrow and your lips become thin?" A joyless Christianity is simply not Christian. The spirit of rejoicing ought to underscore each observance of the Supper, which when rightly entered into is a celebration of God's love for us shown forth in the life, death, and resurrection of his only Son our Lord. Like a birthday or a wedding, the Supper signifies a time for happiness and blessedness. But in the Supper there is a soul-stirring depth of wonder, arising from our glad awareness that it is God who offers us redemption from the guilt of sin and the fear of death, and gives us newness of life through faith in Jesus Christ. This is why, of all the names Christians have given to the Lord's Supper, the Eucharist is perhaps the best.

The sacrament or ordinance of baptism marks the Christian's entrance into the life of faith, as the Supper signifies participation fully in that life. In those churches which practice adult or believer's baptism, the act is preceded by a conscious decision on the part of the one baptized to follow and obey Christ as his personal Lord. In those churches which practice infant baptism, the parents of the child and the sponsoring congregation commit themselves to bring up the child "in the nurture and admonition of the Lord"; and the action is expected to be confirmed by the one baptized when he or she reaches the age of personal decision. Yet in either case the meaning of baptism is response to God's freely given love in Christ, his claiming of his own, his everlasting mercy toward us. Whether the vows of discipleship are taken by the person being baptized, or by the fellowship of Christians on his behalf, baptism is the outward sign of God's grace shed abroad in our hearts through faith.

As we all know, the mode of baptism varies in our churches. Too much should not be made of the obvious differences, which have historical reasons and appeal to different scriptural texts for justification. Common to them all is the use of water and the name of the Trinity; and this gives to baptism a church-wide unity that far outweighs historical separateness or division. Water is the symbol of cleansing and new life, "humble, precious, and clean" as St. Francis of Assisi said. When immersion is practiced, there is the dramatic imitation of that dying and rising with Christ which is the great double movement of authentic faith. When water is placed or poured upon the head of the one baptized, the meaning is that of being named or signed with the blessing of God in Christ. Clearly, there are values in both practices which belong to the fullness of the church.

Why are these two sacramental acts important for the right understanding of the church? Because the church itself is a sacramental fellowship. It draws its faith and life from sources deep within the Being men call God. It models its action in the world upon God's mighty and gracious action as revealed in Christ. It offers up for God's use and blessing the tokens of creaturely human existence — blessings of home and work and companionship — confident that as he has made our flesh his home, so he will lift us into his renewing, saving presence.

More than Religion

In our day an increasing number of voices are calling for a "religionless Christianity." That is, they want to have faith without the complications and compromises of the actual church. They take a dim view of what they term the "establishment" of institutionally based religion. They feel that faith has gotten badly bogged down in organizations, that the gospel is all but lost in programs and procedures. And they point out how completely the churches have taken on the protective coloration of their environment, how closely they are tied into the social and economic scene, how tamely they reflect the worldly values and hopes of our affluent culture.

All this is true to an alarming extent, and it would be folly to deny it. The question is, however, whether the situation can be improved by "traveling light," getting rid of all the paraphernalia of religion. Really, what is at stake in this mounting criticism is the church's own understanding of itself. There can be no doubt that God and religion are not the same; and yet the institutions of religion in the world do bear broken and imperfect, but unmistakable, witness to the presence of the living God in our midst. Here again, the vessel is not the treasure, but the treasure needs the vessel if it is to be maintained against destruction and decay in a world which tends to be forgetful and self-important. The church is certainly a part of what we mean by "religion," yet it also knows itself to be a witness to something infinitely more significant

— the love of God for the world made everlastingly plain in his Son.

How may the church, religious institution that it is, more faithfully and clearly serve God as the place of meeting, where he makes himself known as the Father of our Lord Jesus Christ? That question should have top priority in the minds and wills of church members today. Our determination must be that of obedience to our mission as the people of God. When the church learns to put the will of God first and its own welfare and success second, it is on the right track. "To be to the Eternal what a man's right hand is to a man" — that is what matters finally and supremely.

The Apostle Paul called the church by an unforgettable name: the body of Christ. That is about as "high" a view of the church as can be imagined. It means that the institutions of religion are indispensable for doing God's work in the world, since otherwise it would not get done at all. Yet at the same time Paul's great image means that these institutions are but instrumental to God's powerful purpose and must put themselves at his disposal if they are to be what God intends. If the church is the body of Christ, it is only because Christ is the head of the church. He is the animating and directing intelligence by virtue of which the church exists, moves, and serves in the world. If Christ were not the head of the church, it would be not a body but a mere corpse.

Once again, it is the mystery of the church that defines its meaning. An invisible reality shines through the visible structures of church organization and action even when these structures block our vision. Christ remains the Lord of his church in spite of our betrayals and disloyalties. When all is said and done, our life is "hid with Christ in God." We may think of ourselves as Protestants or Americans or members of some religious organization, but we are first and foremost the people of God's choosing, the servants of a servant Lord.

As we become more aware that this is so, our church-manship is not diminished but greatly increased in importance. We are not to think more highly of ourselves than we ought to think, because the church is only the bodily instrument for doing the will of God. But by the same token the church is to be cherished and strengthened, corrected and renewed, so that it may become an ever finer instrument. Our task in the church is simply that of being useful to our Lord, and there can be no greater, nobler one than that.

It cannot be denied that much remains to be done if the church in our time is going to serve its function well. If we acknowledge Christ as Lord, then we are bound to know him also as our judge. Our latterday scribes and Pharisees, busy with what the world calls religious work, may very well come under the same condemnation which Jesus visited upon the religious busybodies of his own time. To those who will not put first things first in the church, the imperative of Christ is crystal-clear: If your enemy is hungry, feed him; if you want to be forgiven, forgive; be reconciled with your brother if you would be reconciled with God.

Only a church which has the mind of Christ can be the body of Christ. It is by loving our neighbor that we prove the genuineness of our love for God, and of God's love for us. If it is true, as has been said, that eleven o'clock on Sunday morning is still the "most segregated hour in America," then we in the churches are falling far short of what the Lord requires of us. For how may we love God whom we have not seen, if we do not love the neighbor whom we see every day? Where justice for our fellowman is concerned, it seems sometimes as if God could wait for the church no longer, so he acted in the world.

Then, too, there is our own life in the church which needs greatly to be rectified and reformed. Who can suppose, for instance, that denominations or local congregations must be the only true form of the church in our time? If we were to ask what sort of church could genuinely represent God's intention for the present world, would the answer not have to be given in ecumenical terms? How may the work of God get done unless we do it together, in the unity of his Spirit known through Christ?

We might go on to speak of many levels of worship, witness, and work in the church, but I trust the perspective for our speaking is at least clear. Let us affirm, then, that the church exists for the purpose of rendering human religiousness ever more viable and pliable to God himself. Let it be stated once again that whatever meaning church activities or organizations may have is given to them by the mystery of God's deep, enduring love for all mankind. To make the invisible visible is our churchly privilege and obligation; and thus God's living purpose is made known.

What, if the church is to be obedient to God's purpose, should come first on the Christian agenda today? What should come last?

Do you think that the movement toward church union among Protestants is in line with the nature of the church? What are some of the movement's opportunities and dangers as you see them?

Does God act in the world without or in spite of the church? In other words, just how indispensable is the church to God?

Do baptism and the Lord's Supper assist, or hinder, your own experience and understanding of the relationship between Christ and the church?

6

Sacred
and secular

Today it seems as if the sacred has all but disappeared from the scene of our life. The stage on which we play our various roles is this-worldly, no longer other-worldly. Economic pressures, political alignments, social expectations, or personal ambitions are the forces that determine what we are and how we are going to act. Where in all this complicated human pattern of advance and retreat, success and failure, is there any place for what our forefathers called the holy? In the kind of world we know best and belong to, at any rate, there is no supernatural being hiding in the wings, waiting to untie the knots that people get themselves into or to right the wrongs they perpetrate on each other. Many among us have quietly decided that the world is just what we make of it, that we are simply on our own, and that the business of living from day to day is a purely secular affair.

To be sure, the church still exists, rather like a pocket of resistance desperately trying to keep a tiny corner open for God. Somehow it is able to keep alive, just barely, the idea that there is a Maker, Lover, and Keeper of life who brings us into existence, cares about what happens to us, and calls us into his service. But more and more the world goes on its own way unheeding; it marches to the beat of a different drum, leaving religion to repeat its ancient incantations without either hearing or following them. In the centers of power where decisions are made that condition us all, can it be seriously believed that any real concern for what is holy or sacred is in evidence? Or is it possible to hold with honesty that our common life is being lived "to the greater glory of God"?

The Vanishing Sacred

These questions are partly rhetorical, of course; we know, or think we know, the answer in advance. The modern world has little time left for the sacred, and is learning to get along without God in conducting its business. True, traces of Christian faith remain, splendid new churches are still being built, some genuine efforts at revitalizing religion are taking place. But who would dare to say that Christianity generally is in a robust state of health or that it is proceeding with confidence down a purposeful path? The space left open for God is shrinking fast in both private and public life. There can be no doubt that "things are in the saddle and ride mankind," as Emerson said well over a century ago.

Indeed, the secularizing process has been going on for a long time now; it is a distinguishing mark of the whole modern period in our history. It means the gradual but unmistakable movement of men's interests and activities away from the sphere of religious control. Its slogans are "art for art's sake," "business is business," and the like. The Gothic cathedral rising above the clustered roofs of a medieval town or the colonial meetinghouse facing the New England green are charming relics of a Christian past. They once expressed the importance of the sacred in the very midst of life, but they do so no longer.

"Nothing is sacred any more" is a complaint that is often heard nowadays, whether parents are speaking of their children's behavior or old taboos are being flouted in the newspapers. It is easy to share this feeling of shock and disappointment because there are so many things that seem to justify it. Especially to those who have cast their lot with the church, the idea comes naturally that the modern world as a whole has abandoned God and is busy building substitutes for what used to be called the holy.

This is only one side of the picture, however. Actually the churches have been retreating before the secularizing process for a long time. Back in the early 1800's, Sören Kierkegaard was already pointing out how religion had gone on the defensive, retiring to its "fortress" and pulling up its drawbridges leading to the world. Still today many people in the churches feel that the proper business of religion is the cultivation of something called the "spiritual" life, distinct and separate from everything "worldly." These Christians resent and deplore the involvement of some of their fellow members in the controversial issues of public and private morality or in social, economic, or political affairs. They believe with all their hearts that the sacred must be protected and the secular left to itself; and so they contribute mightily to the very secularizing process which they are quick to condemn. As the churches are restricted to the purely religious realm they become more and more an isolated segment on the fringe of modern life, so that the world seems left without God, and God seems left without the world.

Hence the church in our time often seems to be a kind of Christian ghetto — picturesque perhaps, but largely without a shaping or moving force with respect to the world's ongoing life. If this impression is at all true, it raises the sharpest possible questions as to how the living God can be known today, not only by the world but by the church.

All Life Is God's

In all the talk about the waning authority of the church or the disappearance of the sacred from the scene of life, there is often far more heat than light. Much of our Christian confusion and anxiety comes from what is really a wrong assumption. That is the notion that the sacred is a realm set apart, somewhere on the other side of normal human existence. This way of thinking sees the modern secularizing process as threatening the sacred, which therefore needs protection and preservation by the church. If we do not do this work of cherishing and guarding, who else will? Whether the issue has to do with prayer in the public schools, Sabbath observance, or the sanctity of marriage vows, the attitude is the same. The churches tend to regard themselves as the caretakers of the sacred, fighting a battle against great odds to keep intact — that is, "pure and unspotted from the world" — whatever may be deemed high and holy.

Some of the oldsters among us can still remember an American institution known as the "front parlor." When houses were more spaciously built than they are today, there was usually an extra room where the family heirlooms were kept. It remained shut except on significant occasions like a wedding, a funeral, or the annual meeting of the Ladies' Aid Society. But at such times the doors were thrown open and the front parlor came alive as a vital part of the house. Between times it was simply there; its contents were not to be touched or rearranged; the room was being held in readiness for its very special uses.

Isn't this rather like the "Sunday-best" conception of religion with which many Christians are still trying to work in the face of an increasingly secular world? Their idea is expressed in songs like "Take Time to Be Holy" or in the motto about the little plant of reverence that needs to be watered once a week. This is not wholly wrong, of course. If there were no special time and place set aside for "the deep things of God" they would soon be forgotten and ignored altogether. Realizing this, every human culture has found ways to treasure and preserve what is regarded as sacred, in shrines or temples or through particular events

77

and writings. But once the proper vessel has been made to hold the treasure, it becomes natural and easy to go on refining and elaborating the vessel rather than to point beyond it to the treasure for the sake of which it really exists. Something like this has happened in the Christian churches of our time.

When good Pope John was asked what was the purpose of the reforms he supported in the Roman Catholic Church, he answered by going over to a window, opening it wide, and letting in the fresh air from the outside world. A better symbol for what is needed in the life of all our churches could hardly be imagined. Confronted on every hand by the pressures of a world which does not know Christ and could not care less, the church which is embodied in our churches must abandon its postures of defensiveness in order to show that all of life, not merely religion, belongs to God. Religion is only that part of life where the whole of life is claimed for him, just as Sunday declares the true meaning of the rest of the week.

Nearness to God does not involve keeping one's distance from the everyday concerns and responsibilities belonging to our human lot. The secular is not the enemy of the sacred, but its God-given field of exercise and opportunity. Martin Luther said it well: "The sphere of faith's works is worldly society and its order." Just so; and the church is therefore called upon to venture forth boldly and eagerly, in God's name to claim all of life for him.

Instead, then, of building higher and higher walls between the secular and the sacred, Christians ought to be in the business of discovering the sacred in the midst of the secular. That is because our faith acknowledges no limits to the power and wisdom of God. We believe him to be the source and the goal of everything that exists. We do *not* believe that he is the God only of those who believe in him. Nor do we believe that God restricts himself to those experiences, activities, or groups where we expect to find him. Nothing can be exempt from the guarding, guiding, governing love of God as he is disclosed in Jesus. On the contrary, everything can serve as token and bearer of his presence and holy will.

For holiness first of all means wholeness — the wholeness of the world under God. It does not mean separation or division, but rather the breaking-in of the divine upon the world, so that the world becomes the sounding board and mirror for the divine. God alone is holy, but he communicates his holiness to everything that is his. As Scripture says, he dwells in light unapproachable; but it is in his light that we see light, and we really do see. It is no accident that all the great religions of the world, including Christianity especially, find in this symbol of light a very meaningful image for the holy or sacred. Light is everywhere, inexhaustible; light is not so much what we see as why we see at all; and light penetrates the darkness, bringing unity and clarity into whatever is confused or obscure. Hence, in the words of Scripture, "God is light, and in him is no darkness at all." We live and move and have our being, not merely from God and toward God, but in God; our relationship is not to Someone "out there" or "up there," but to the Beyond that is within.

All life is God's, and so the distinctions we are wont to make in our religious perspective do not apply to him. This is the Christmas message of the Incarnation, of God's entering our world in humble human flesh. In Christ he comes to make the whole of life holy. He does not visit us from on high, like a brief meteor flashing in the night sky. He takes our bone and muscle, our guilt and striving, for his own. Before God in Christ instituted his church, he had made the world his home. That is, he was in the world by the power of the Incarnation, and the church arose in grateful response to that fact. Any attempt on our part, therefore, to shut him up in our sacred vessels is doomed to failure. Just because he is the world's true Lord he is also Lord of our faith.

It follows then that our task is to discover and release

within ourselves the same openness to the world and freedom for the world that God expressed in Jesus Christ. It is not we who must give him to the world; it is he who gives us to the world and the world to us. He has gone on before us into the world, showing us how to share his love for the world, and giving us on every hand tokens of his advancing presence. To follow Christ is to pursue him in his own identification with everything that human living involves and means. It is to see in every man the brother for whom Christ came, taught, healed, suffered, and died. It is to love my neighbor as Christ has loved me. It is to take the circumstances and choices of life as they come, meeting them in the confidence that God in Christ has made them into opportunities for my faith, hope, and love.

Thinking from Below

This arresting phrase is used by Colin Williams in his book *Faith in a Secular Age*. It is a good one to describe the way of looking at ourselves and the world which results from the secularizing process. The rapid growth of science is largely responsible for this. Science has accustomed us to thinking of our human capabilities and possibilities as arising "from below," that is, in our animal inheritance and wholly within our natural environment. We do not look today, as our Christian forefathers did, to such terms as "soul" or "spirit" to explain what man is and how he acts. If we want such explanations we turn rather to psychology and sociology, which are based on natural sciences like chemistry and physics. Higher forms of life are to be understood in terms of the lower, later in terms of the earlier, and more complex in terms of the more simple.

Thinking from below also operates in other ways. It is frequently remarked that we live in a technical age, although the meaning of such a statement is not always clear. We can readily see that we are surrounded by an abundance of machines and mechanical processes, but this is not merely a matter of adding techniques to the same world as before. The fact is that the world itself is very different. The machinery of a few generations ago extended the range of man's control over his environment. A human operator worked the pedals and levers, stepped in to repair or correct, and remained visibly in charge. Today, however, this human element is greatly lessened. Someone has said that as the technical revolution took over the work of the human hand, the computer revolution has taken over that of the human brain. Instead of extending man's control and realizing his purposes, a giant computer makes man seem unnecessary and even obsolete. We may as well face it: in a technically dominated world like ours, man is forced to ask himself what being human really means. What can he do that a machine cannot do better?

It seems that a new kind of man is being born in our technical, secular age. This new way of being human accepts the picture of the world that science gives. It does not explain changes in the weather, for instance, by referring to the action of an angry or a friendly God. It wishes to eliminate as much as possible the holdovers of magic and superstition that used to be bound up with faith. It places the burden of human betterment on man himself, insisting that our problems can be solved if we will only analyze and tackle them. Whereas men formerly thought that the "real" world was superior to this one, because it was supernatural and divine, the new man of our time believes that reality must be found in the here-and-now of ordinary experience with its challenges and possibilities.

Thinking from below is evidently here to stay and there can be no going back to thinking from above, downward from God to man and nature. We must accept the fact that something serious has happened which cannot be obliterated or reversed. The question for Christians, therefore, is whether the living God can be known any longer in the ways hallowed by tradition and adopted for so many centuries. That question has already been asked in earlier chapters of this book, and it will arise again. Right now we are meeting it in connection with the sacred and the secular. What is happening to the old, familiar world of holy places, persons, things, and times? If the sacred must be discovered in the midst of the secular, how are we going to detect its presence?

Before trying to answer the question in earnest, it is important to set the stage and the terms on which it can be answered. If we simply let the secularizing process tell us what and how to think, then of course we have given up trying to answer; or rather, we have answered in advance and so have not even heard the question. But if we only repeat worn-out, very tired answers, then we have not heard the question either.

If people do not find God disclosed in the middle of life they are not likely to look for him at the top or bottom of life. Dietrich Bonhoeffer, who has been mentioned before, wrote that a God who appears only at life's extremities where man feels weak is of no earthly use unless he also can be found "in the midst" where man feels strong and confident. This is certainly so for most of us today. In Bonhoeffer's phrase, "a God of the gaps" whom we meet only at the limits of our knowledge or our energy will no longer do.

There is a story about an ocean liner which was rolling badly in some heavy seas. A lady passenger came anxiously up to the captain to ask how serious the situation was. "Madam, we are in the hands of God," was his somewhat pious reply. "Oh," the passenger gasped, "is it as bad as that?" People today are not likely to be much impressed by appeals for faith in God which take their weakness, ignorance, or frailty for granted. They prefer to believe that God has something to do with the good, strong things of life. They do their thinking from below.

And surely we should understand this and respect it. The "far-off look" is not widely prized or shared at the present time. It does little good to keep on telling people who do not have it that they must acquire it. Neither can we suppose that if people can only be made miserable enough they will automatically turn to God, for they might just as well turn away from God altogether. No, the case for God must rest upon more solid and secure foundations than that. The case must be made by life itself, by evident and indubitable experience, and of a positive rather than a negative kind.

Thinking from below, however, is not particularly friendly toward any religious interpretation of life. Indeed, it goes on with a very real sense of liberation from all such viewpoints. There is one world, and man is the meaning of it. To many people in our time this insight comes with an exhilarating, freeing force. It is morally bracing to realize that men and women themselves are responsible for what they make of history. Dark, demonic powers are to be feared no longer. So-called higher, divine authority is conspicuous by its absence. "The fault, dear Brutus, is not in our stars, but in ourselves that we are underlings," as Shakespeare wrote. Is not the meaning of our secular age that the world is set free to be itself, sheer world, without needing to appeal to or escape from any other world than this?

The Sacred, New Style

How can the sacred or holy be in evidence in such a picture of the world and of man's place in it? One might readily suppose that a secular world like ours would see no need for God or holiness. Yet we have already said that from the Christian viewpoint all things, whether the world calls them secular or sacred, belong to God. Can this viewpoint be justified and shared today?

Well, certainly nobody is going to be argued into believing in a God he cannot find for himself. Men are persuaded by what they know to be true rather than by thoughts which have occurred to the minds of others. Unless God appears "in the land of the living," as the biblical phrase goes, he is not likely to mean anything at all.

Another point worth emphasizing is that a God who confined himself to what men had decided to call sacred would simply not be the God of Abraham, Noah, Jacob, the prophets, or Jesus of Nazareth. Such a God would in fact be an idol, manufactured by religion and kept high on the shelf for special purposes of reverence and praise. He would be there when he was needed, but safely out of the way when men must be about their nonreligious business. The living God of genuine faith, however, is not so accommodating. He smashes the idols men would try to trap him in, and insists on putting in an appearance where men would prefer to be let alone. The sacred may well call attention to God; indeed, that is its rightful function; but it had better not pretend to contain him.

"The sacred in the midst of the secular" — that, as indicated earlier in this chapter, is the direction in which our eyes of faith should look today. There is no denying that it will be difficult for some of us at first. It will be like coming out of the dim religious light of the church into the glaring, blinding light of the world. But it will not be the first time that new wine has burst old wineskins or the treasure of the gospel has overflowed its customary vessels. Often in the past the Spirit's leading has taken us far out beyond known frontiers and familiar scenes, and it is doing so again.

There is a Christian understanding of the secular as well as the sacred. This means that "thinking from below" does not forbid but in fact demands an interpretation in the terms of faith. Hard as it may be, this work of Christian thought must be taken up and followed through.

It was a nineteenth-century German philosopher, Friedrich Nietzsche, who first took up the cry so often heard today that "God is dead." Significantly, he put this announcement into the mouth of a madman who went on to say, "And we have killed him." Nietzsche's idea was that the whole drift of modern life in its secularizing process had abolished God from the stage on which we play our parts. His declaration has been revived at the present time by those who feel a similar experience of absence and loss.

But what if this so-called death of God in our time has *not* been caused by man himself? Is it not just possible that God has not so much been expelled from the world as he has removed himself for reasons of his own? Perhaps he is teaching us how to get along without him in the old way, and is urging us to adopt new ways of approaching him. And is this experience of God's absence so very different, after all, from that of Jeremiah, Job, or Jesus himself when hanging on the cross? As it finally deepened and increased their faith, may it not also strengthen ours?

"Earth's the right place for love: I don't know where it's likely to go better." These words of Robert Frost define our Christian vision and task for the world of today. Our business is to accept now a new life in this very world of skyscrapers and computers, of rapid change and revolutionary conflicts, of massive movements and private anxieties. The name of that new life is "love"; and love means being open to another as if his need were our own, as if we counted equally before God. It means doing and being for our fellowmen what God did and was for us in Jesus Christ, his Son, our Lord. It means entering boldly and gladly into the secular arena where lines of hostility are being drawn and where taking sides becomes inevitable. It means accepting suffering or misunderstanding in order that God's will may be done on earth as it is in heaven.

Our kind of world, more than any other before it, makes it abundantly clear that life means life together, that a man lives only insofar as he gives, and becomes whole only in relationship to others. "We are entangled in the bonds of love and cannot escape, struggle as we may." In such a world we may easily pass Christ by without noticing him, but he is there all the same. For he is in the brother and the neighbor, and in us insofar as we serve the brother and the neighbor. "As you did it to one of the least of these my brethren, you did it to me" (Matthew 25:40). No time, more than our own, has made it possible to see and serve the holy God in the midst of the common life. Its very style, secular as it is, discloses the true meaning of the sacred. Nostalgia for what is far-off and long ago has no real place in it.

Yet openness to one another in the world is only possible if the world itself is not closed tight against the incoming God of love. This must be our Christian word to all who are content to think from below.

According to Christian faith, God may be present in his very absence. The one thing of which we can be sure is that he will continue to take us by surprise, speaking to us when and where we least expect to hear him. And that, of course, is precisely because he is a living God.

Secularism is sometimes termed "man's new religion." How do you interpret and respond to this statement?

What kinds of evidence do you see for, or against, the author's view that "thinking from below" is widespread at the present time?

A well-known theologian recently remarked that America is at once the most religious and the most secular nation in the world. What does this comment mean to you?

To what extent can you accept the author's idea that God may be teaching us to get along without him in the old, familiar way, through living in a secular age?

7

The world
God so loved

When someone says, "the world," what meaning do you hear? To some, the image of a globe comes to mind with oceans and continents drawn on its surface, river systems and mountain ranges indicated, national boundaries sketched in, and varieties of temperature and climate suggested. To an astronaut orbiting high above the planet Earth, this meaning of "world" might make real sense. A rounded whole, apparently complete in itself yet with amazing diversity as well, a place of human habitation and of natural resources — this would express for many people the chief meaning of "the world."

But to others this picture of an earthen ball spinning around the sun is far from being the whole story about the world; and we Christians are among them. It is not so much that geographical, political, or economic ideas of the world are false, but are they true enough? What of the other planets in our solar system and of the distant galaxies many millions of light-years away? Modern science has vastly enlarged our picture of the world, or rather of the universe, in such a way that imagination is stretched to the utmost and thought breaks down. At last, it seems, we have attained a vision of the world that is worthy of the God in whom we believe, an open universe of nebulae and incredibly remote stars in which our planet Earth is but a tiny speck of speeding light.

And yet this may be just the trouble — that our faith in God does not keep pace with our exploding knowledge of the universe as science discloses it to us. If faith remains tied to the apron strings of a view of the world that is obviously false, then our God is indeed too small to matter much to men and women today. The writers of the Bible took for granted that the earth was flat and covered by the starry sky like a great tent, above which God dwelt in his heaven, and that beneath the earth was located the place of departed spirits. This earth, they believed, was fashioned out of chaos by an almighty Maker whose will was its eternal law. But can this belief be honestly shared any longer by people who know "what the score is" with respect to the findings of geologists and astronomers in our century? Does not the new knowledge make it difficult if not impossible to believe in God the Maker of heaven and earth?

So, while the knowledge of an expanding universe does provide our faith in God with a fitting and significant setting for both Christian comprehension and commitment, it also strains and even shocks our faith because it makes necessary some far-reaching and long-overdue changes. That is a situation no honest Christian can escape. The only way out of the situation would be to keep faith and knowledge in separate compartments, like the man whose right hand did not know what his left was doing. That however would destroy the integrity of the person and ignore the unity of truth itself. It would be every bit as offensive to faith as to science. There must be, and there is, a better way. We must wrestle once more with the truth of science and of faith, convinced that they are at bottom one.

A World — Created

There was once a pastor who had the habit of preaching every year a sermon on the latest discoveries in astronomy.

This perplexed some of his parishioners who came to him to ask why. They wanted to know what possible good this annual lecture could do for people who made their living by working in offices, stores, and factories. The pastor replied, "I don't know, but it greatly enlarges my idea of God." He had a real point, of course. Just because God is infinitely greater than any idea we may have of him, our ideas are in constant need of revision and enlargement. And nowhere is this more true than in the matter of our knowledge of the world for which we Christians believe that God is ultimately responsible, as its Creator and Lord.

Therefore, when we declare that we believe in God, the Maker of heaven and earth, as our forefathers did, do we really mean it? Or are we merely repeating a time-worn, handed-down opinion? The answer is important, for much depends upon it. Among other things, the possibility of knowing the living God is at stake. Clearly, it is not enough for vital faith to know that there was once a God, or that our ancestors believed in him; such knowledge is "for information only" and cannot engage our minds and hearts.

Knowing the living God, whatever else it may mean, must have something significant to do with the present world in which *our* living happens. Is this the kind of world in which the thought of God as Creator still has force and substance for our minds? In view of what we are being told about the long processes of evolution, about ourselves, and about outer space, can we still speak with positive assurance concerning the created world?

Yes, we can and should. Creation is not a theory of how the world began, to be discarded as soon as a better theory comes to light. Neither is creation offered by the Christian faith as an attempt to explain such order as we find in the world in terms of a cosmic mind, although it has sometimes been used in such a hypothetical way. What creation means, centrally and chiefly, is that this is God's world — to be understood and lived in as owing its very being to a source and purpose other than its own. The universe, or rather many universes, probed by science is not made by God in the way that a carpenter makes a box, nor even in the way that an artist paints a picture. God is surely not a craftsman who takes the materials at hand and shapes them by his skill into a useful or beautiful article. But the whole of things by which we are surrounded and within which we exist cannot explain itself in its own terms. What we call "the world" points at many levels and in many ways beyond itself. Our knowledge, however impressive and important, is always running out into final mystery. We do not know enough about the world, or perhaps we know too much, to be able to do without God in our thought and life.

The Christian doctrine of creation means that we are creatures and that ours is a creaturely life. In other words, we human beings are not self-explaining any more than nature is; we ask about the why and wherefore, the whence and whither of our life; we are marked from top to bottom and from first to last by the sense of our creatureliness, of our dependence. Nowhere has this sense been stated more finely or beautifully than in book 10, chapter 6, of the *Confessions* of St. Augustine:

> "And what is this God?" I asked the earth, and it answered, "I am not he"; and everything in the earth made the same confession. I asked the sea and the deeps and the creeping things, and they replied, "We are not your God; seek above us." . . . I asked the heavens, the sun, moon, and stars, and they answered, "Neither are we the God whom you seek." And I replied to all these things which stand around the door of my flesh: "You have told me about my God, that you are not he. Tell me something about him." And with a loud voice they all cried out, "He made us." . . . And I turned my thoughts into myself and said, "Who are you?" And I answered, "A man." For see, there is in me both a body and a soul; the one without, the other within . . . But the inner part is the better part . . . For the truth says to me, "Neither heaven nor earth nor anybody is your God." . . . But your God is the life of your life.

Old legends of a ready-made universe produced by a divine artist-workman may indeed have lost their force today. But the experience of creaturely dependence so tellingly evoked by St. Augustine still rings true. In the words of the Bible, "It is he who has made us, and not we ourselves." As ours is a creaturely life, so ours is a created world.

A World of Things

There are some people, a very few in the entire human family, who have claimed to know God directly and intimately. Such people are called mystics. For most men and women, however, the knowledge of God is mediated by the world in which it happens. In fact, this is a large part of what creation means. Thus God gives us life through our parents, energy and light through the sun, and entertainment through a clown in the circus. The Creator and his creation are not the same, as St. Augustine makes clear in the passage quoted above. Yet the Creator can be known through what he brings into being and sustains in being, just because the world is his. Everywhere about us we have signs and tokens of his creative abundance and aim, "letters from God" as the poet Walt Whitman wrote.

The apostle Paul, in his correspondence with the church at Rome, expressed this thought in simple, unforgettable words: "Ever since the creation of the world his invisible nature, namely, his eternal power and deity, has been clearly perceived in the things that have been made" (Romans 1:20). Here once more we come upon the basic distinction between what is visible and what is invisible, as we did in thinking earlier about the church. To the eyes of Christian faith, everything that is seen is a shadow cast by what we do not see. Since most of us are not mystics who can claim to have a direct vision of God, we must be content to discover in the visible world what may be called the trademark or signature of its creation, that is, its God-intended and God-guided nature.

As Scripture says, God has not left himself without a witness in the world. That means that nature is not to be taken merely for granted, as it appears on its surface, but as capable of pointing beyond itself in the direction of God. So for Noah the rainbow served as a sign of God's promise to him and his descendants. So for Moses the mountain called Sinai witnessed to the high and holy purpose of God's law and covenant. And so for Jesus the flowers of the field were expressive of a glory greater than King Solomon's. To live in faith is to be aware of nature in a new way, to see things from a new angle of vision which does not diminish their reality but rather enhances and deepens that reality.

People who do not go to church very often are sometimes heard to say in excuse that they prefer to "find God in nature." While we may perhaps disapprove of using this phrase as an alibi, we should at least admit its measure of truth. A golf course or a superhighway may not, indeed, be the best place to discover God, and yet the possibility should not be entirely discounted. It just might happen there. At any rate, God has not left himself without a witness in our places of travel and recreation, or of work and family relationships. God does not have to be spoken of or consciously served in order to be present; and we are not at liberty to suppose that he can be known only where and when we are seeking him deliberately.

Our knowledge of God through the things of nature is indeed indirect, not immediate; but it may be genuine and significant for all that. Do I not know my best friend in similarly indirect, refracted ways? It is by means of the letters he writes, the sounds he utters, the gestures he makes, that I discern his real intentions toward me. I have no possible way of seeing into him apart from the medium through which he chooses to make himself known. I cannot even have that sort of direct knowledge of myself except through images in a mirror, bodily sensations of pain or pleasure, and other signs belonging to the world of things. If this is true of personal and interpersonal know-ing, how much more true it is of our knowing God through nature! And yet we should not hold such knowledge cheaply when it is the most solid and reliable knowledge we can have.

This is a far cry of course from saying that nature is itself divine. God is not "in" nature as a plant or a planet is. If he were, then he would not be what we Christians mean by God, but what the Hebrew prophets called an idol. Neither is God identical with nature as a whole, according to the Christian faith, since this would imply that creation and the Creator are the same. Men have sometimes spoken of nature in personal terms, calling it "Mother," for example. Thus they have attempted to express their dependence upon nature without seeing that nature, too, depends upon God. Their efforts, we might say, have gone much too far in the right direction. It is well and good to see "through all this fleshly dresse/Bright shootes of everlastingnesse," as Henry Vaughn wrote. But it is something else again to suppose that nature and God are simply two words for the same thing. That supposition has no place in our Christian way of looking at the world. The story of creation as we have it in the book of Genesis shows God in his freedom standing before, above, and over against the world he has created.

Yet for all that, God's creation of the world is understood by Christian faith not in terms of sheer difference and dis-tance, but as an act of incomparable love. Because it is orig-inally and finally God's, the world in every part and as a whole is "very good" in his sight (Genesis 1:31). A British poet of the last century, Gerard Manley Hopkins, spoke of a "dearest freshness deep down things" which marks them with the signature of God's love. "The world is charged with the grandeur of God," Hopkins wrote, because it testifies to the outgoing and self-giving love which is but another word for creation. The fact that there is a world at all bears wit-ness to God's being-for-others, his will not to remain shut up within himself but to go forth and share his being by creating an object for his love.

The Christian understanding of the world as creation binds together nature and human nature, things and persons, in a most profound way. St. Francis of Assisi knew this when he wrote so lovingly about "our brother Sun" and "our sister Moon" in his great hymn of praise to God for giving man the world. To be sure, such an awareness of kinship is difficult for us to attain nowadays; the bulldozer, skyscraper, and airplane have seen to that. Perhaps, indeed, one of the best ways to restore the knowledge of the living God among us would be to reawaken our slumbering sense of the world of things as the "garment of praise" that gives eloquent tribute to its Creator's love. There is a familiar hymn which expresses this sense well in speaking of God:

> Center and soul of every sphere,
> Yet to each loving heart how near!

A World of Persons

When we turn from the natural to the human world, the possibility of knowing God becomes both greater and more remote. This is because persons, unlike things, have wills of their own. Things may be seen in faith as reflecting God, but persons are capable of responding to him. However, the human power of response is free, that is to say, determined by the self who gives it, and so may either accept God or reject him. God has not brought us into being as puppets whom he can control or coerce into loving him. He has "made" us in the image of his own freedom, taking the full risk of our saying "No" to him. His love wants our love in return; but he will not compel it, for that would only mean the denial of love. The surest sign of his love is that God gives us the ability to turn away from him, treating us like children and not like playthings. He would not have it any other way. He would rather take the chance of our disobedience and mistrust than to leave us wholly without any freedom of our own.

In the biblical story of creation it is written that God made man in his image or likeness. This does not mean that man is a copy or replica of God, only smaller and weaker. What it does mean is that man is basically, essentially free. He has power to choose, and to do what he chooses. He is not the mere result of influences and forces that shape his experience, but may by his decisions weave them into a life-pattern that is uniquely his own. The great painting by Michelangelo on the ceiling of the Sistine Chapel in Rome shows God extending his hand to the outstretched hand of Adam, thus establishing living contact between the finite and the infinite through freedom. This is a stirring symbol for the Christian truth about man in his relationship of response to God.

When we try to say what God is like, our thoughts turn naturally, and indeed inevitably, to the best in our humanity. This is not to pretend that God can be measured on the same scale with man, or that he is more of the same only greater and better. But how else can we know God except by means of what we know in ourselves or others? That is part of the burden of our creaturehood, but also part of its privilege and glory. Whenever we see resolute purpose despite heavy odds, or joyous enthusiasm, or quiet dignity on a suffering face, we are entitled to say, "God is like that." It is in human qualities such as these that we discover reliable clues, real glimpses into the loving character of God.

The fact is that men are not always at their best. They may use their freedom to go against God rather than to accept his Lordship in their lives. This means simply that we must do our seeing of God "in a mirror dimly," as Paul wrote (1 Corinthians 13:12). Yet this is far better than having no mirror at all. If God is love, then he is best revealed to us through beings created capable of entering into a loving relationship with him, even though they neglect or misuse that capacity. To refuse love is at the same time to bear witness to its reality, perhaps more forcefully than if love were accepted. A child may pout and fret because his mother denies him something he wants, but he does not thereby diminish or erase his mother's love; he only affirms it by his misunderstanding of it. When human freedom goes sour in selfishness, the image of God in man is certainly marred, though by no means obliterated.

Therefore it is right to look for God's likeness in our own lives, however short they come of what they are intended to be. The truth is, man is a spirit as God is Spirit, and that is the bond of likeness between them. The difference, however, is that man receives while God gives. Where man is weak, he looks to God for strength; where man is strong, he has his strength from God.

Two small boys were playing one day with their father's steel tape measure. They were so fascinated with it that they invented a delightful game of guessing the distances between things in the house and then checking their guesses by measuring with the tape. How many inches is it from the sofa to the fireplace? That was guessed, then settled by applying the tape. How many inches from the window to the lamp? From the front hall to the kitchen? As the distances measured grew, so did the boys' confidence. Finally the younger one, carried away by his enthusiasm, asked, "How many inches do you think it is from here to the moon?" The older boy replied, with contempt edging his voice, "How crazy can you get? You don't measure that kind of distance in inches. It's too big. You have to measure that kind of distance in feet!"

That is a good illustration of the sort of problem we always confront when we use human measurement to arrive at the knowledge of the living God. There is a common measure in the truth that our lives open out upon the mystery which faith calls God, "in whom and through whom and to whom are all things." And yet whatever contact and communion we may have with God must be by

way of spirit touching Spirit across the mighty distance
caused by human sin. That kind of distance is not measured
finally by man at all, but by God in his love declared
through Jesus Christ our Lord.

Without trying to capture the ocean in a cup, or to
measure divine distances in human inches, we still believe
that the world of persons affords an indispensable kind of
access to the knowledge of the living God. In human personality and community we are provided with creaturely
models of God's loving intercourse and will to fellowship
with us. Where would our faith be without words like
"Father," "Kingdom," "Spirit" — all drawn from what we
know of man?

A World — Loved

To many Christians the heart of the gospel is to be found
in John 3:16: "For God so loved the world that he gave his
only Son, that whoever believes in him should not perish
but have eternal life." The verse which follows is equally
important: "For God sent the Son into the world, not to
condemn the world, but that the world might be saved
through him." These verses have such a firm hold on our
hearts and minds because they say so clearly that the relationship between God and the world is centrally one of
love. The whole reality in which we exist, things and persons alike, is here declared to be the object of God's delight
and concern. No more sweeping or far-reaching statement
could possibly be made on behalf of Christian faith. God
"has the whole world in his hands," and as he brings it into
being, so he purposes to save it from peril and destruction
by the power of his everlasting concern.

It is not because the world is lovable that God loves it.
The writer called John has a great deal to say in his Gospel
concerning the darkness that is in the world, about the way
in which it turns away from God and causes tribulation to
the faithful, and about its stubborn preference for evil

rather than good. In fact the very word "world" in Scripture often has the meaning of that which is against God and resists his saving, renewing will. All through Christian history there have been men and women who accepted this negative judgment on "the world," seeking to escape its contaminating influence and to find in religion that peace which the world cannot give.

Yet the world, no matter how unlovely, is loved by God, and Jesus Christ is the sure proof of that. Since when did love wait to be assured of the worthiness of its object, or need to be returned before it was given? No, love is spontaneous and generous, utterly free and careless about demanding its own due. It can bear and believe and hope in spite of everything. God is like that, says our faith, and this is the manner of his approach to us in Christ.

There is judgment in such love because no one wants to be shown up in his lovelessness toward God. Love, as John's Gospel puts it, is a light fingering and penetrating the world's darkness. It reveals the darkness for what it is. But the darkness cannot put out the light. God's own world may not receive him, but that does not stop God. He dares to put himself at our disposal knowing that we may resist or reject him. He does not call us to a grim accounting but makes himself our way and truth and life. So man's age-old search for righteousness is swallowed up in God's forgiveness. In Christ, God makes himself like us in order that we may be made like him. Thus the hard grip of sin is broken, fear and guilt before God are destroyed, and even death loses its sting.

What does this mean for our life in the world? Just this — that now we live in an entirely new world, whether we are ready to confess it or not. Old things have become new; the rough places have been made plain; the high have been humbled and the low have been exalted. The world itself is different, and our situation in it is different as well. It has been penetrated and enlightened by grace and truth so that even in its restlessness and weariness we may find durable direction and unflagging purpose as well as ultimate joy.

There is a common saying that it is love which makes the world go around. We Christians would prefer to say that it is love which renews and reinvigorates the world, like the coming of spring after a long, hard winter. What God in Christ offers to the whole world is the power of new being, of being new. And he does not merely hold out such a possibility before us while waiting for us to meet its conditions; instead he enters lovingly into everything we call our life, making common things holy and weak things strong.

And it is not as though we had this precious truth shut up within our faith, which then we must convey by our missionary strategy to an unbelieving world. God's deed of love has been already done, his gift in Christ already given. He is in the world by the power of incarnate, serving, suffering, and reedeeming love. We do not have to bring him to the world; he is there before us. Our task is rather that of recognizing in the world God so loved "the fit habitation of the Most High," witnessing on every hand to his determination that no one should perish but that all should have everlasting life. More than anything else, God asks of us that we love his world as he loves it still.

In what ways and to what extent should our exploding knowledge of the universe influence and change our inherited understanding of God?

In the Psalms, the world of nature is often said to "praise God." What meaning can this have in a scientific age like ours?

How may we believe that "the world is loved by God" when there is so much evidence of evil and suffering in it?

8

Knowing and doing the truth

Most of us pride ourselves on being very practical men and women. We have little time for theory, unless it has something to do with improving methods and conditions in our busy, active lives. Being where the action is matters more to us than having a clear and correct understanding of the world in which action happens. Our questions have more to do with the how than with the why of things. So it is not surprising that where matters of Christian faith are concerned we want to be assured that faith can be put to work, that it makes a real difference to the way we actually live.

This is all very well, provided that we keep our balance and do not go overboard in one direction only. There are times for careful thought and times for decisive action, and they have more to do with each other than we often suppose. While it is certainly possible to become so intrigued by mere ideas that the business of life remains undone, it is also easy to get so involved in mere doing that we lose our sense of direction altogether. If understanding without doing is empty, doing without understanding is apt to be blind.

Obviously, we need both doing and understanding if we are to be whole persons.

Knowing and Doing

The Gospel of John has much to say about knowing the truth, and promises that this will make us free (John 8:32). At the same time however this Gospel emphasizes that whoever does the will of God will know the doctrine of his revelation and redemption in Christ. Here again it is made plain that knowing and doing belong together in the life of faith, that each requires and completes the other.

In this book, up to now, we have been mainly interested in reaching a better understanding of the living God. The stress has been on knowing rather than doing. But by itself this emphasis is insufficient unless it can show us what and how we ought to do to make our knowledge vital and practical. We are entirely right in demanding this of any treatment of the Christian truth about God, because that truth above all other kinds of truth is something to be done as well as known. In fact, the only way in which it can be known is by being done.

"Why is it so hard to believe? Because it is so hard to obey." Thus Pascal speaks for all of us. His words mean that before we can grasp the truth about God with our minds we must commit ourselves to him with our wills and hearts. Right believing is always the fruit of right living. Likewise our difficulty in believing comes as much from moral hesitation as it does from mental blocks or problems. To obey is hard indeed, especially when it requires a drastic change in our old habits and attitudes. All the same, obedience is what it takes to loosen up resistance, liberate us from our fears of being made new, and open wide our eyes for the seeing of God.

In our attempts to bring up our children as growing persons of sound character we understand this well enough. We do not try to teach them everything they need to know and then expect them to act wisely upon it. They are assigned small duties and definite responsibilities before being given a larger share in the family's work and welfare. We think, and rightly, that our children will learn the truth about themselves and others as the outcome of active experience. We do not expect them to know first and act afterwards; it must be the other way around.

Can it be otherwise where knowing God is concerned? We are all children when it comes to understanding his will for us and for our world. No one of us can honestly claim to have arrived; all of us are hopefully on the way toward clearer and fuller knowledge. This means that we are lifelong learners in the school of life, seeing here a little and there a little more, depending upon our readiness to listen and obey. "The spirit must practice its scales of rejoicing," writes a modern poet, just like a child sitting down to his piano practice. Faith, hope, and love are given by God, to be sure; but these qualities are given to be learned and practiced.

The key word in practical Christianity is the word obedience. In love, God cuts and fits his truth to our condition, challenging and encouraging us at the same time. He does not ask us to do what is humanly impossible, but he expects us to realize what is possible. His gift of truth has a peculiar way of shaping itself into a task, indeed many tasks, to be undertaken by those who would be faithful and loyal to his leading.

Obedience is in some ways a hard word, and what it stands for is harder still. Acting in advance of knowledge, or in the absence of complete knowledge, is never easy, although it is exactly what we are doing all the time. Yet we should not suppose that this means stumbling blindly through life as if no direction signals had been provided. We may not have all the truth we want, but we have all the truth we need in order to act.

Nor should we think that obeying God is like snapping to attention before some human authority who may punish us if we do not. Obedience to God is not a mere reflex of fear, or if it is we have not learned our Christian lessons very well. To obey God is most of all to put our trust in him, doing the truth we know, and letting God take care of the outcome. It means handing over the controls of our lives to the Creator and Governor of all life, following the prompting of the Holy Spirit as he guides and sustains us in what we do.

Again, it would be very wide of the mark to suppose that Christian obedience consists in observing rules or executing commands. "Theirs not to reason why, theirs but to do and die" is no description of our life with God; our human freedom and intelligence are much too precious and useful to God for that to be allowed to happen. Actually, when we come to think of it, obedience is not to rules or commands at all, but to a person whom we have good reason to trust. To obey is to put ourselves into another's keeping, to give up trying to be our own boss, and to do the other's will instead of ours. There are imperatives in the gospel, surely, but they take the form of great life-patterns and not finicky, detailed codes of behavior. When we try to make them over into rules and orders for the minute regulation of life, we simply squeeze every bit of the majesty and mystery out of them.

The wish that Christianity should be made practical is an entirely laudable one, provided that it does not result in a Christianity that is only a set of laws for regulating the traffic of life. We do well to remember how the prophets and Jesus spoke out against this kind of degradation of faith in their day. To be truly practical is to be obedient unto God, waiting upon him, learning how to listen to his voice still and small in our hearts, and then daring to commit our wills and our ways to him.

When I was a boy my father tried to teach me how to play baseball. He gave me this advice: "Keep your eyes on the ball, and your hands will take care of themselves." There is a similar kind of counsel in the gospels regarding Christian practicality. "Seek his kingdom," said Jesus, "and these things shall be yours as well. . . . Where your treasure is, there will your heart be also" (Luke 12:31, 34).

KNOWING THE LIVING GOD

Doing Is Love

The Jewish world into which the gospel came was one in which conventional religion had become largely a matter of observing laws laid down by God. In this way it was thought that righteousness could be attained. Jewish life was regulated from top to bottom by this vast network of divine commandments. No one could possibly keep them all or even know what they all were. But one could always try harder the next time, inching his way little by little toward God's approval and reward.

When Jesus of Nazareth began teaching and healing, after being baptized by John the Baptist, the people soon became aware that his good news about the God of love was noticeably different from the older forms of Jewish righteousness. More than once he challenged those guardians of the Law, the Pharisees, and earned their hatred as a result. To them he seemed disrespectful of the Sabbath, careless in deportment toward non-Jews, and a rebellious troublemaker who deserved the condemnation of righteous people. This disturber of Israel's peace, they felt, was certainly not the promised Messiah his followers claimed he was. He was rejected by many because of his apparent disregard for the Law which had been established ever since the days of Moses, and which had become a kind of religious security system guaranteeing the relationship between God and his chosen people.

Jesus, however, thought of himself as a Jew and remained one for all of his brief life. When he was asked to account for his unsettling behavior and beliefs he replied that he had come "not to destroy but to fulfill" the ancient Law of Moses and the prophets. He resisted every attempt to cast him in the role of a revolutionary leader. At the same time he was obviously far more interested in men's inner motives than in their outer behavior, and like the great prophets before him, he insisted upon the crucial importance of an attitude of faith in contrast to performing correct works and duties. He had a most uncomfortable manner of turning the Law back upon its zealous advocates, showing them up for what they were, sinners all, and calling into question their very notion of righteousness before God.

Years afterward, the Apostle Paul found himself caught between the Jewish communities and the new fellowship that had sprung up around Christ, or as he himself put it, between the Law and the gospel. He said that the Law once had its place as "a schoolmaster to bring us to Christ": but now that Christ had come, the gospel superseded it. What Christ had done was to break down the "wall of partition" between God and men, and also the necessity of climbing over that wall deed by deed, righteous act by righteous act, until God's favor had been gained. As Paul saw it, God himself had come to us in Christ, making our very flesh his home, and wiping out by his sacrificial death any lingering debt which we might still owe to God. Instead of righteousness, the work of man, forgiveness as the work of God has now been made the way and the truth for human living. Instead of trying harder to earn favor with God by observing his commandments, we are to accept God's forgiveness, which of course means also accepting ourselves as we are, and then to open ourselves to God's incoming and indwelling Spirit.

Surely we must side with Paul and not with the Pharisees in believing that because of Jesus Christ, righteousness has been swallowed up in forgiveness. For us, too, the old reign of the Law is at an end. Faith is no merit system or stepladder of human achievement; it is receiving and then sharing God's freely given love in Jesus Christ our Lord. Oddly and sadly enough, there are still some Christian Pharisees who would make faith a matter of law and love a duty instead of a delight; but that can only mean that the gospel has fallen on deaf ears, that some are still engaged in climbing up the old wall (and falling down again) rather than in taking God at his Word and living on his promise of grace through faith. Nevertheless, whenever the gospel is truly proclaimed and obediently heard, it is the good news that God has done for us what we cannot do for ourselves, enabling us to abide in the love with which he loves us.

It is not surprising that to some the gospel simply seemed to be a new version of the Law, but now called the law of love. That is man's inveterate habit in things religious. It is not to be denied, however, that Jesus himself went along with the Jewish understanding of love as the supreme law of religious and moral conduct. The story told by Luke makes this abundantly clear:

> And behold, a lawyer stood up to put him to the test, saying, "Teacher, what shall I do to inherit eternal life?" He said to him, "What is written in the law? How do you read?" And he answered, "You shall love the Lord your God with all your heart, and with all your soul, and with all your strength, and with all your mind; and your neighbor as yourself." And he said to him, "You have answered right; do this, and you will live" (Luke 10:25-28).

The lawyer had rattled off the required statement correctly, and Jesus agreed with him that this was indeed the condition for obtaining eternal life. Evidently there was nothing more to be said.

Nevertheless, the lawyer persisted, unwilling to let the matter rest. He asked Jesus for a definition of the neighbor, and Jesus told him the parable of the good Samaritan. Thus Jesus took love beyond the realm of law, of rights and duties, altogether; his parable did not evade the lawyer's question but rephrased it and turned it back upon itself. Jesus, here as always, presented love in terms of a claim upon our obedience, as an imperative to be acted upon; and yet how different it is in the parable from any merely moral or religious duty! In the response of the Samaritan to a fellow human being's need, there is no effort to "get right with God" but only spontaneous sympathy for a suffering man which leads unhesitatingly into action taken on his behalf.

Here, as in Jesus' own living and dying, the Law is not so much destroyed as it is fulfilled. But having been fulfilled it is no longer necessary in the old way, that is, as a command from on high keeping men in line with God and at their proper distance from him. By the love of God that was in him Jesus fulfilled the law of love, and by his love for us he gives us power to become loving men and women. In Christ, love gives what it commands and realizes what it requires. It makes itself superfluous as law because it has become available, through faith, as "life of our life," to quote the words of St. Augustine.

How strange it is, then, that we should go on talking about "applying" the gospel as if it were a matter of attaching love to our life from the outside or cutting ourselves to fit its pattern. Not application but appropriation, taking the gospel into ourselves by faith, is what is really called for; and we are assured of the presence of God's Holy Spirit among us for just this purpose. Only accept the fact that you are accepted by God, as Paul Tillich put it, and God will begin to do his work of love in you. Or, in the words of Christ himself as told in John's gospel, "Abide in me, . . . apart from me you can do nothing. . . . As the Father has loved me, so have I loved you; abide in my love" (John 15:4-5, 9).

And to all this one can only add those further words of Jesus, reported in many passages of the New Testament: "He who has ears to hear, let him hear!"

Love for My Neighbor

In the Jewish summary of the Law, the love of God comes first and is spelled out in detail while the love of the neighbor seems tacked on, almost as an afterthought. That is the form in which the lawyer recited it to Jesus. One of the most striking things about Jesus' own teaching, however, is that love of the neighbor comes first, not perhaps in the order of final importance but in the order of immediate doing. If we do not love the neighbor whom we see every day, asks John, how can we possibly love God whom human eyes can never see? Or if one has a grudge against his neighbor as he goes to the temple to pray, then he had better make things right with his neighbor before daring to approach God's presence.

This certainly suggests that Jesus gives neighbor-love a real priority over the love of God, at least so far as human urgency is concerned. Did he actually intend to reverse the ancient Jewish order? What is the meaning, really, of his insistence upon the prior claim of the neighbor on our loving?

We often tend to think of Jesus as a great idealist who saw undreamed-of possibilities in man and gave us the blessed assurance of God's grace in realizing them. That is true enough to a point, but we should also see how much of a realist Jesus was in his estimate of human wrongness and self-centeredness. He knew what was in man, as the Bible emphasizes, and that means sin and fear no less than grace and freedom. Is it not just possible that Jesus' constant emphasis on loving our neighbor has its basis in his unsparing realism with regard to our natural inability to love him?

At all events, if we are to be true followers of Jesus, we can hardly separate our love for God from our neighbor who stands before us needing such love as we can give him. We are only deceiving ourselves if we say we have love for God in our hearts when our neighbor cannot rouse the slightest spark of love in us. The point of Jesus' teaching — and example — is that these are not two different loves but one and the same. We cannot love God without loving our neighbor too; and we cannot love our neighbor without also loving God. Here, of course, Jesus echoes and confirms the best in his own Jewish faith.

This is why any attempt to separate the "spiritual" from the moral and social claims of the gospel has to be rejected, as being both unchristian and unhuman. Compartments are fine in a kitchen cabinet or a post office, but in living the Christian life they are out of place. Our responsibility to God is one with that toward our fellowmen; the one depends upon the other, deeply and inevitably. We must have our love in both ways or we shall have it not at all.

Who is my neighbor? This is the question the lawyer put to Jesus, presumably expecting an abstract definition, only to get a story of true neighborliness instead. In the light of the parable of the good Samaritan it becomes altogether plain who our neighbor is: anyone in need, anyone whom we can help. His ancestry or present circumstances or status in the community does not matter. Our own preferences or past associations or social expectations do not matter either. All that matters is that a fellow human being is in some sort of trouble which we have the power to alleviate. In the parable, of course, the neighbor is someone who is visible and whose plight is obvious. But in the conditions of our modern life there are many neighbors, in the gospel sense, whom we do not know directly and shall probably never meet in face-to-face encounter. How may we be neighborly toward them?

It was a bishop of the Church of England in the last century, Charles Gore, who said, "Love is the ability to read statistics with compassion." In other words, love always particularizes, individualizes; instead of categories and stereotypes (Catholic, Communist, criminal, or what not) it sees persons like ourselves. Labels are useless when it comes to loving. They are even worse than useless, because they give us so many phony alibis for not loving, or for packaging and restricting our love. There are real differences between men and they may not be totally disregarded, of course, but these do not constitute any reason for withholding Christian compassion from them. Love is an effort of the human imagination, which sees right through the smoke screens of this world's tiresome, incessant classification and generalization, its neat and easy disposal of the man or woman who is our neighbor behind the barriers of prejudice and provincialism. Love is the triumph of the human and the humane over everything that is inhuman, unhuman or subhuman.

The ancient Jewish law regarding neighbor-love, which Jesus inherited and brought to fulfillment, had in it a great amount of realism about man's moral shortsightedness. Thus it ran: "You shall love your neighbor *as yourself.*" That is where the rub comes; to advise us to love the neighbor might seem to be enough, but the law digs in deeper; he should be loved as each of us loves himself, and that is something else again. We know full well that self-love is a fact and does not have to be commanded. All right then, said the law, love your neighbor just as much, at least as much, as you love yourself. In practice, this means not putting yourself in another's place (we do that all the time, and with what dire results!) but rather putting the other in the place you normally give yourself. That, as Thomas àKempis said, is "a most praiseworthy, manly thing" to do. Yet it does not come naturally to us, and so it has to be commanded. Jesus took this "as yourself" and made it the life-pattern of his whole work on earth. We who call ourselves Christians must be prepared to go and do likewise, following the example of his great humility and his God-given humanity.

The Door to Knowing

So let us be as practical as we can about this matter of loving the neighbor as we love ourselves. For one thing, let us get rid of the idea that loving someone means liking him. Of course it is a great boon when these come together, so that our affection for and our responsibility to the neighbor strengthen and sharpen each other. But if we begin by describing the neighbor as somebody we like, we have already made it quite impossible to love him in the way the good Samaritan loved the man whom he found wounded and left half dead by the road. How many neighbors we have in the human family whom we cannot like because we do not even know them, yet who are given us by God to love! Love is really not a way of feeling at all, although it helps to have the right feeling toward our neighbor; it is above all else a way of doing and of being, that is, of bending our life into the shape of someone else's need.

A first and one of the surest tests of love, in the Christian meaning of the word, is that it can be extended to someone who is unlovely and unworthy. This is why the test case in Jesus' mind is that of forgiving our enemies. Our neighbor the enemy — that is the sort of human situation in which nothing but love can really motivate any action taken in his behalf. To go "all out" in love toward somebody who has done us harm or wishes us ill, to make his good our own in our conduct toward him, is about as pure a case of unselfish concern as can be found. Here at least one cannot be suspected of using the neighbor-enemy or getting something out of him; loving can hardly be confused with liking in this case. Perhaps that is why Jesus mentions it so regularly as expressing the meaning and bearing of love for life lived in his spirit.

Secondly, let us clear the decks for the practical business of loving by recognizing that in God's sight all men are equal. No one can claim special privileges or superior status before him. This is the meaning of the hard saying in the New Testament that "God is no respecter of persons." Our human distinctions and divisions, on which so much appears to hang, are "foolishness with God." Differences of heritage, environment, or opportunity make no difference to God. He sees each one of us for what he is and loves us all for what we are — and may become, by his grace. The masks we wear before each other are dropped before God. The ways we sort and rank ourselves seem strangely flattened out in the divine presence. Thus to carry them into the worship of God is actually to commit an especially sinful kind of blasphemy, perhaps even idolatry. While we compare ourselves to one another, usually to our own religious advantage, God must find these proud comparisons just a bit amusing, to put it mildly.

The only one who can afford to be condescending in his love is God, and he has chosen in Christ a very different course. He chose the way of the cross. Thus he showed us the depth and riches of his love — how far down he was willing to go with man, and how abounding, free, and utterly gracious is his disposition toward us all. We are not God, but he has given us his Spirit to strengthen us by might in the inner man, in order that in our own turn and sphere we may express that same love.

In the third place, and in the light of everything we have been saying, let us emphasize again that doing God's will is the door to knowing him. He who loves is born of God and knows God. There is really no other way except the rocky, risky way of loving our neighbor as God loves him and because God loves him. Not all the learning in the world, nor all man's heaped-up good intentions, nor even his fleeting glimpses of what is supremely worthful, can outweigh one little ounce of real loving. God has given each of us our neighbor — every man — to love, and he has given us the power of loving him in Christ.

If then we would clear our vision for the seeing of God, let us remove the hindrances and obstacles to loving our neighbor. In his teaching Jesus employed the humorous (and shattering) illustration of the man who was so busy trying to get a speck out of his neighbor's eye that he could not notice the beam that was in his own. Whatever in our own shortsightedness prevents us from seeing our neighbor as he is to God, whatever in the world keeps us from serving his good as if it were our own, must go. The truth that frees us for love is to be done before it can be known; and it is in the doing of that truth that it makes itself known.

If God is love, as Jesus Christ taught and showed us, then it is love which he requires of us. That love is our human means of knowing him. Let us make no mistake about it: doing in love what truth demands is the plain meaning of the gospel. Indeed, it is the only way in which the gospel can have any meaning at all.

It has been remarked that the true opposite of love is not hatred, but indifference. Do you agree or disagree? Why?

Read over 1 Corinthians 13 in the light of what is said about love in this chapter. In what way does Paul's view either confirm or call into question that presented here?

How would you answer, in contemporary terms, the question asked of Jesus, "Who is my neighbor?"

Does the author pose the contrast between love and Law in too sharp a fashion? How would you prefer to state the way in which they are related in Christian moral experience?

9

Therefore choose life

This book began with a question: How may second-hand faith become faith at first hand, that is, faith founded on a knowledge of the living God? In successive chapters we have endeavored to give answers to that question. First of all, we looked at "knowing" itself in its many meanings and methods. This was necessary in order to get off to the right start, avoiding misunderstandings and possible disappointments. Knowing God, we said, is more like knowing persons than observing facts, because our own commitment and involvement are essential.

Then we spoke of Christ as the Mediator through whom God has declared and bound himself to us. It was pointed out that in Jesus of Nazareth God chose to give the supreme expression of his incomparable love for all mankind. We saw that in him who is the human face of God we are shown the meaning of God's love. Thus Christ is our best, our surest clue to the lovingness, the loving nature of him whom we call God. We found in the Bible an indispensable witness to God's gift of himself in Christ, and so we called Scripture "the mirror of the Word" which opens up our own unending, living dialogue with God as we encounter him in faith.

The church, that strangely mixed reality of divine treasure and earthly human vessels, concerned us next. Created by the call of God yet maintained through the fidelity of men and women like ourselves, the church is forever in danger of putting its welfare first and God's saving purpose second; but when the church is obedient to the mission of its Lord it becomes again the place of God's appearing the living witness to truth which has been made known or which is yet to be made known among us, for the world's sake.

In the chapter on the meaning of sacred and secular we expressed the conviction that these are not departments or segments of life, but differing ways of regarding all of life. The Christian faith holds firmly to the sacredness of the secular, on the ground that all life belongs to God so that he may be known in any part of it. Surprise is what can be logically expected when we have to do with a living God.

Then we moved toward the world of things and persons, inquiring how God's love for the world is shown and known by what we see in nature and humanity. The answer given was that the world is rich in creaturely models and images of God's wisdom and power, which enable us to start from wherever we are and to read the world in the language of faith.

The chapter preceding this one found us saying that knowing God is fundamentally a matter of doing his will. There is no shortcut to such knowledge which can avoid the path of obedient action. Only by loving our neighbor as ourselves can we open our eyes to the love of God which is all around us; doing in love what truth requires is our whole business as Christians, as it is our Father's business, too.

There really is not a great deal more to say. A book like this can only go so far; when the reading is over the living must begin. It may be helpful, though, to survey the ground which has been covered, in order to gather strength for the leap ahead. Two main themes have been sounded and repeated in the preceding chapters. The first has to do with the priority and initiative of God himself. "In the beginning, God" applies not only to the creation, but to every moment of our existence as persons before him. Knowing God is not like discovering some new star in the heavens, nor like mining the earth for silver and gold. That is, God is not to be known by our own efforts at searching him out, however well-intentioned or reverent. It is God who makes himself knowable by moving toward us, putting himself at our disposal, speaking for himself in the language of our experience. Without waiting for us to pry his secret from him, God wills that we should know him and calls us to the place of meeting with his Word.

The second theme concerns man's part in arriving at the knowledge of the living God. This is chiefly an alerting and opening of our hearts and minds to the signs of his presence. Just as a photographic plate is sensitive to light, so human beings are created capable of responding to the promptings of God. But we forget, and need to be reminded. We bury our talent for knowing God beneath the surface of everyday preoccupations and involvements. We allow our taste and zest for God to go unused for lack of exercise, just as we forget who we are in the rush of our many chores and commitments. Therefore our part must largely be that of removing self-made obstacles between us and God, of breaking through the crust of our self-centeredness so that God can get his Word in, can be listened to and heard.

This might be enough by way of summary, but we are practical people who want to plan our course by means of guidelines and directives. While there is no guaranteed technique, no single method, we are right to want whatever help we can get in order to make use of the resources lying at hand. How then may the insights we have shared in this book become part and parcel of our manner of life from day to day?

Making Love a Habit

A phrase in a familiar gospel song, "if your heart keeps right," makes an important point. It indicates that love must become a habit — a settled and determined attitude resulting in a consistent course of action. That is the only kind of love that makes any real difference to our neighbor or ourselves. We may even say that it is the only kind that actually counts with God. Good intentions or sympathetic feelings are fine, but unless they are harnessed and put to work they serve no better purpose than that of paving the road to hell, as the old adage goes. The heart needs to be kept right.

We Christians are not without guidance for the training of the heart in the habit of loving. Men and women have faced these problems before us and have found answers that worked for them. They may not all be our answers, too, yet they deserve a hearing and a try. Obviously, we shall need all the help we can get in the schooling and training of the heart for "love's redeeming work."

First, consider what it is that has to be disciplined into loyalty to Christ — the heart. Usually when this word is mentioned today it brings to mind what William James called "the feeling side of life." Popular songs and romantic poetry encourage us in this. The heart becomes a kind of shorthand expression for the turbulent realm of emotions and affections in which so much of our inner life is spent. To speak of disciplining the heart, then, suggests taking action against one's own unruly wants and needs, subjugating rebel territory by a process not unlike that of military invasion and pacification by some alien power.

But if we were to read our Bibles more carefully we would soon discover that "the heart" means something quite different there. As a man "thinks in his heart, so is he," the writer of the book of Proverbs tells us. He further warns us to keep our "heart" with all diligence, for out of it "are the issues of life." Here the heart stands rather for

117

the centered wholeness of my being as a human self; it means, quite simply, my own me. Feeling plays a large part in making me the sort of person I really am, of course, and I underestimate this at my peril. But thinking, willing, acting are important factors too, and none should be disregarded, for all yield expressive clues to my own selfhood, my own being as a person.

The training of the heart, then, is nothing more nor less than self-discipline. For this there can be no short-cuts, panaceas, or substitutes. It is a job which we must do ourselves, and it will give us steady work throughout the extent of our lives. The apostle Paul knew this very well. "I pummel my body and subdue it," he said, comparing his life in Christ to that of an athlete in constant training. He was under no illusions about his own impulses and desires; he knew that they often got in the way of his obedience to the Lord of love. And on another occasion he spoke of the life of faith as bringing "into captivity every thought to the obedience of Christ" — a long, hard exercise indeed.

Paul's understanding and practice of the Christian life as watchful, strenuous self-discipline commends itself to us all. He was not interested in spiritual muscle-building for its own sake, but for the sake of "running with patience the race that is set before us." He knew that he must take and keep himself in hand if he would not be disobedient to "the heavenly vision." Because of what God had done for him, there was something he must do for God; and it was necessary to remain in condition, in a state of constant readiness, if that task were to be accomplished.

In this light consider the famous chapter on love in 1 Corinthians 13. Sometimes it is called a "hymn to love"; yet while it is true that love is praised in the chapter, it would be better to say that it is a description of love in practice as a working habit.

> Love is patient and kind; love is not jealous or boastful;
> it is not arrogant or rude. Love does not insist on its

own way; it is not irritable or resentful; it does not rejoice at wrong, but rejoices in the right. Love bears all things, believes all things, hopes all things, endures all things (verses 4 to 7).

Notice clearly that in Paul's view love is not a single virtue to be imitated but a whole pattern of attitudes and traits ranging from simple courtesy to deliberate compassion. Notice too that all the expressions of love of which Paul speaks have to do with our bearing toward our neighbor, and represent on our part a steady resolve to put the neighbor first in our attention and concern. And notice, finally, how Paul describes love by saying what it is not, thereby indicating that love does not come naturally even to followers of Christ and so must become a matter of continual, habitual effort.

Making love a habit does get easier, however, when we take advantage of those ways and means developed by the church in response to its Lord's great imperative. Only as Christian purpose becomes Christian procedure does our membership in the kingdom of love take on the genuineness of real commitment. It is for us, as Romain Rolland has said, to "think like men of action, and to act like men of thought."

One such method is the practice of prayer. You may remember Coleridge's ancient mariner declaring:

> He prayeth best who loveth best
> All things both great and small.

But that is no excuse for not praying; it is in fact the best possible reason for "continuing instant in prayer." When we have to deal with the man or woman who is our neighbor whom God has given us to love, we often do not see the neighbor for what he is. He may seem to be a nuisance, a hindrance, or a cog in the machinery of self-advancement. But if we pray about our neighbor, we take time to picture him, to see him from the inside as we see ourselves. We ask what he would want from God if he were in our place. Here we are thinking of what is called intercessory prayer

— that is, prayer which pleads on behalf of another. There can be no question that such praying deepens the habit of love in us, for we try to form an image of the neighbor as he must appear to God, and then offer up our request on his behalf.

Man's original sin is perhaps not so much selfishness as it is lovelessness. They may amount to pretty much the same thing, to be sure. And yet the reason why men use others to get whatever they can for themselves is simply that their sense of the neighbor to be loved for his own and for God's sake is so poorly tended that it dies of discouragement. This is where the prayer of intercession may help. Not asking what we want for our neighbor, not telling God what we would do if we were our neighbor, but pleading with God to give us light and strength to serve our neighbor — this is bound to decrease and break up the habit of not loving. And the more frequent and deliberate such prayer becomes, the greater are the chances of our being worthier instruments of God's love.

A second method appointed by the church for softening man's stubborn hardness of heart is that act in public worship called the offering. Granted that our churches spend the larger part of money received in this way on their own support and self-improvement; yet is it not still true that the offering does represent at the heart of worship the claim of neighbor-love upon the Christian? Yes, for it is a regular and purposeful action taken by a congregation which provides the means of loosening up the crust of human self-sufficiency and self-concern. An offering may only be perfunctory or automatic, but it does not have to be so. Skilled and sensitive participation by pastor and people alike may mean that the offering is a true "lifting up of the heart."

The taking of an offering in a church service is a kind of acting-out of Christian stewardship at the visible and corporate level. What we do there is a sign of what we should be doing all the time. How emphatically our Lord Jesus teaches the meaning of stewardship in parable after parable! Thus it is made plain and vivid that we are servants of a servant Lord, that we are entrusted with what we have for the purposes of love. John Wesley put this unforgettably when he said that all our life is "lent to be spent."

Prayer and stewardship are but two of the many ways in which we Christians are alerted to the need of the neighbor and to our responsibility to meet that need. These regular and expected habits are not ends in themselves, of course, but means for doing God's will on earth as it is done in heaven. And beyond these responses at the level of habit there will always be other, unforeseen demands for sympathetic involvement in the lives of our fellow men and women. The whole point of building up love through habits of self-discipline is that we shall not be caught unprepared when God's love puts us on the spot of immediate decision and urgent action. Then, rooted and grounded in the ways of love, we may be sure that God will "fit our charity with circumstances" worthy of our calling.

Maturing as Christians

The meaning of our life, according to the gospel, is that we are made by love and for love. This meaning, however, is not something that can be grasped all at once or realized in a single flash of illumination from on high. It dawns upon us gradually, for the most part, through day-to-day experiences and encounters which may seem at first to have little if anything to do with faith in God. Then, as we come to acquire more competence in caring, and as our normal craving for love from others is more and more supplanted by ability to give love to them, a way is opened up which leads ultimately toward God himself.

It is a sound principle of all education that learning depends upon readiness. We are not interested in blurting out the truth in a take-it-or-leave-it manner, hoping against hope that some of it might chance to lodge in a mind here or a heart there. But we are mightily interested in helping persons, younger or older, to move surely ahead on the path of Christian maturity by nourishing and strengthening the learner at each stage of his growth.

There was once a Roman Christian lawyer, Tertullian by name, who declared that the whole aim of church education was to produce "a soul naturally Christian." If what he meant was that growing persons should be allowed to glide easily and gradually into full obedience to Christ, he was plainly wrong, for that is not how it happens at all. But if he means that people must be taken where they are and met on their own ground so that faithful love becomes the very air they breathe, he was certainly on the right track. Experienced educators tell us that imposition and indoctrination of meanings which are alien or premature can only result in uncomprehension, perhaps even in resistance. This is hardly the effect desired by preaching or teaching in our churches.

In one way or another, what all of us are interested in producing is change, not only in belief but also in behavior. What is the good of preaching or teaching if people remain just as they were before they heard the liberating Word of God? Obviously, the gospel asks men to change their lives — not to make minor adjustments here and there, not to say "Lord, Lord" without doing the things the Lord plainly requires, but to be born again, becoming new in the strength of the good news of the gospel.

Yet far too often we assume that merely telling people what we think they ought to do or become is enough. Not long ago an advertisement appeared on many billboards urging people, "Put your faith to work every day." That makes it seem very simple, doesn't it? But it is not that easy. A wise bishop once remarked that it may not take much of a man to be a Christian but it takes all there is of him. And we may add that becoming a Christian is a lifelong task. An indispensable key, therefore, to life-changing faith is to be found in human growth itself. The whole person in his whole development must be touched, engaged, and guided. The kingdom of God, Jesus said, comes not by talk but by power.

Since this is so, it is of great importance that we should not expect man-made miracles of overnight change to result from teaching or preaching. Least of all should we rely on any conversation, book, or sermon to achieve what only God can do. We may plant and water the seed of faith, but it is God's grace, freely given and received, which gives the increase. Men are changed, if they are changed, by God's working silently and mightily within their hearts. Even if it could be supposed that a full set of blueprints might be furnished whereby human life can be patterned after God's intention, it would still be up to God to realize that ideal.

All the same, the power of God to change lives is a proven Christian fact. He reveals himself to those whom he chooses, that is true, but we can and should be ready for his revelation when it comes. There is no need to be discouraged, but every reason to be confident that God will take us just as we are and shape our growing lives according to his purpose. Our work, then, is to work together with God, taking our cue from what we know of him in Jesus Christ and following his lead through the tangled paths of the world.

We hear a great deal in these days about "man come of age" in an environment from which God is conspicuously absent. It is assumed that God must decrease in order that man may increase. But what, pray, does this kind of maturity achieve? A world without God is a world that is less than human. To speak of man reaching maturity in such a world is to confuse responsible adulthood with touchy, self-concerned adolescence. Christian maturity, on the other hand, means "to grow up in every way into him who is the head, into Christ" (Ephesians 4:15). Far from being a declaration of independence from God, it is a constant, deepening reliance upon him for attaining "the measure of the stature of the fulness of Christ" (Ephesians

4:13). Mature manhood is not a state of arrival but a style of approach, an "upbuilding in love."

No Christian can ever claim to have achieved maturity, but he can point with confidence to a process of maturing going on, a "growing up into Christ" which is taking place in himself. As Paul emphasized so strongly, this is not a matter of boasting at all, nor of comparing oneself with someone less advanced along the road of Christian discipleship. It is rather in the nature of a testimony and a thanksgiving to God who "gives the increase." And the signs of this maturing will be found in a gentling and humbling of ourselves, a greater willingness to make our neighbor's good our own, a more eager readiness to move out of self-encirclement toward him in genuine and unhindered love. The fact that this does happen in spite of everything, that we can still learn new traits and habits, is of all the things that can be said about man the most heartening and hopeful.

It cannot be assumed, of course, that once this maturing process has been described it will automatically come to pass. Words have many important properties, but the magical transformation of human character is not among them. Yet some words can better reach and grasp "the heart" than others. While it may indeed be true that ultimately Christian characters cannot be taught but only "caught" by contagion from person to person, it is also true that this process may be helped along by right interpretation and verbal encouragement. We must not expect language to do something of which it is incapable, yet neither should we despair of its life-changing power altogether, especially when it is closely joined with sincere and honest action in the speaker's or writer's own life.

Growing up into Christ, therefore, is chiefly the work of God's Spirit within and among us; but it calls for our cooperation and consent at every stage along life's way. Without us the Spirit could not do his work; for if the gospel is the seed of Christian growth, our lives must be the soil in which this growing happens. Christian maturity, just because it is our lifelong task, is our everyday business and concern as well.

Choosing Life

In the first letter of John there are two sentences that finely sum up the message of this whole book: "Beloved, let us love one another; for love is of God, and he who loves is born of God and knows God. He who does not love does not know God; for God is love" (1 John 4:7-8). It is in this intimate connection between knowing and loving that the clue is to be found for a living knowledge of the living God.

Loving and knowing come together in living. They are centered in what the Bible calls "the heart" — that is, in the springs of motive, the inmost space of personality which is the self. There may be many things we can learn about God by hearsay or remote report, but we really do not know him until we have received the spirit of love which comes from God alone and felt his gracious touch in terms of human welfare. It is when the seed of God's love has found its mark in the soil of man's heart, and only then, that we may begin to "bring forth fruit with patience."

Separation, hostility, mistrust all chart the path toward death. Men die a little every day insofar as they go their own way unheeding, closing their hearts against God's call to serve the needs of the neighbor and the brother, until finally they cannot hear the call to love at all. People may take our affectionate concern for granted, or do us wrong either consciously or unconsciously, or act as though we did not exist. Then we become resentful and self-pitying, returning spite with spite and coldness of manner with hardness of heart. Who can blame us for responding thus? Must we not conclude that all the talk about Christian love is unrealistic, nonsensical, or positively stupid?

Yet here it is set down in our faith that he who claims to love God but hates his brother is a liar, and that only he who loves his neighbor as himself can know who God is. Sharing, caring, bearing one another's burdens, and rejoicing in each other's joys, all mark the way to life with God. The only proof of this assertion is in trying it on for size, living it out, letting it grow and gain visible and active shape throughout the whole range of responsibilities and relationships, whether small or great.

God seems dead indeed when our love is asleep or impotent. But God comes very much alive when his love has its way with us, healing and helping our fellow men and women in the spirit of Christ our Brother. Then we know as we are known, and Christ calls us not servants but friends. Therefore, choose life!

> *A recent writer has said that "love and justice are the same thing" according to the New Testament. Thinking especially of the parables of Jesus, do you believe this to be true?*

> *In your experience, does it seem true to say with the author that "knowing God is fundamentally a matter of doing his will"?*

> *What evidence do you see that the church today is putting its own welfare first and God's mission for the world second?*

> *What has been most helpful to you in studying this book? Least helpful?*